THE POWER OF MIND AND CONSCIOUSNESS

by

Vee Van Dam

SKOOB BOOKS PUBLISHING
LONDON

First published in parts by
Vee A.K. Van Dam and SPIRAL PUBLICATIONS
Text © Vee A.K. Van Dam 1986, 1987, 1991.
Copyright © SKOOB BOOKS PUBLISHING LTD. & SPIRAL
   PUBLICATIONS 1991
Series Editor: Christopher Johnson
Design: Mark Lovell
All rights reserved

Published by
SKOOB BOOKS PUBLISHING LTD.
Skoob Esoterica Series
19 Bury Place
Bloomsbury
London WC1A 2JH

ISBN 1 871438 01 2 Paper

Typeset in ITC Garamond by *Shades & Characters Ltd.*, Glastonbury.
Printed in Singapore

CONTENTS

INTRODUCTION ... 1
THE POWER OF CREATIVE VISUALISATION
FOREWORD ... 3
CHAPTER 1— YOUR CREATIVE POTENTIAL ... 4
  1 — Are You Creative?
  2 — Simple Visualisation Techniques
  3 — The Use of Meditation
  4 — The Natural Way
  5 — Ideas
  6 — The Unfoldment of Ideas
  7 — Giving Power To Your Ideas
CHAPTER 2— CREATIVE VISUALISATION ... 20
  8 — The Act of Seeing
  9 — Projecting Thought-Forms
  10 — Holding the Image in Your Mind
  11 — Manipulating the Image With Your Mind
  12 — Hearing the Sounds
CHAPTER 3— GETTING ORGANISED ... 32
  13 — Feet on the Ground
  14 — The Vital Experiment
  15 — Planning
  16 — Setting Up
  17 — Working
  18 — Learning from Experience
  19 — Structural Thoughts
  20 — Application
  21 — Economy v. Risk
  22 — Looking at all the Aspects of an Enterprise
  23 — The Logical Choice v. the Intuitive Choice
CHAPTER 4— CREATIVE INSPIRATION ... 48
  24 — The Spirit
  25 — The Solar Deva
  26 — Extra-Dimensionals
  27 — The Real Face Behind the Mask
  28 — The Seven Planes

CHAPTER 5 — THE ESOTERIC ASPECTS 55
- 29 — Life as an Evolutionary Unfoldment
- 30 — Spirals Within Spirals
- 31 — Gradually Incarnating...
- 32 — Part of the Cosmic Network
- 33 — The Peace Within
- 34 — Other Levels of Consciousness
- 35 — Joy!

APPENDIX — NEW AGE ETHICS IN BUSINESS AND POLITICS
59

MEDITATIONS

- 01 — Introduction 65
- 02 — Meditation Primer
- 03 — Being in Tune
- 04 — Some Simple Meditations

CHAPTER 1 — THE PLANETARY ECO-SPHERE 75
- 1 — Trees
- 2 — Earth
- 3 — Sky
- 4 — Human State
- 5 — Deva State
- 6 — Fusion State
- 7 — Super-Nature

INTERLUDE 1

CHAPTER 2 — THE SOLAR SYSTEM 105
- 8 — Venus
- 9 — The Planets of the Solar System
- 10 — The Sun
- Interlude 2

CHAPTER 3 — THE HIGHER SELF 114
- 11 — The Master-Self Within
- 12 — Megatypes
- 13 — Cosmic Jokes, and Cosmic Questions
- 14 — Meta-Programming Factors
- 15 — The Source of the DNA Bio-Component

INTERLUDE 3

CHAPTER 4— THE CHOICE OF PATHS 124
  16 — The Path of Serenity
  17 — The Path of Creativity
  18 — The Path of Power
INTERLUDE 4
CHAPTER 5— POWER MEDITATIONS 132
  19 — Nature Meditations
  20 — Abstract Meditations
  21 — Cosmic Alignments
INTERLUDE 5
CHAPTER 6— THE BRIDGEWAY 144
  22 — The Extra-Terrestrial Factor
  23 — Individual Channelling
  24 — Group Channelling

JOURNEYING— A WAY OF SELF-DISCOVERY
  0 — Prelude 152
  1 — What is Journeying?
  2 — The Difference between Journeying and Imaging
  3 — Psychic Protection at the Outset of a Journey
  4 — Psychic Protection during a Journey
  5 — Psychic Protection at the End of a Journey
  6 — The Choice of a Journeying Target
  7 — Spiritual & Psychic Alignments During Journeys
  8 — The Channelling Element in Journeying
  9 — The Combined Energy of a Journeying Group
  10 — Journeying from the Point of View of a Channel
  11 — Journeying from the Point of View of the Group
  12 — Invoking the Oneness of the Journeying Group
  13 — Psychic Interference
  14 — The Beginning of a Journey
  15 — The Unfoldment of a Journey
  16 — The Choice of Doorways
  17 — Approaching a Journeying Target
  18 — Landing on a Journeying Target
  19 — Exploring a Journeying Target
  20 — Individual Perception
  21 — Group Perception

III

22 — Periods of Silence in the Channelling
23 — Promptings
24 — The Invoking of Specific Symbolic Keys
25 — The End Stage of a Journey
26 — Returning From a Journey
27 — Grounding a Journey
28 — Making Sure Everyone is Back
29 — Special Cases
30 — The Sharing of the Journeying Experience
31 — Closing Down the Chakras
32 — Disbanding
33 — The Lasting Effects of Journeying
34 — The Creative Potential of Journeying
35 — The Spiritual Significance and Usefulness of Journeying
36 — Higher Types of Consciousness Projection
37 — Transcendence through Journeying

APPENDIX I — THE SEVEN PLANES & THE SEVEN COSMIC PLANES	196
APPENDIX II	197

A— Stars as Spiritual Beings
B— The Local Family of Stars
C— The Unseen Stars
D— Human Beings as Stars
E— The Evolution of Spiritual Beings
F— A Cosmic Master Plan

APPENDIX III — GLOSSARY OF TERMS	204
A COMMUNICATION	208
BIBLIOGRAPHY	212

THE POWER OF MIND & CONSCIOUSNESS

INTRODUCTION

Herein you will find three books — THE POWER OF CREATIVE VISUALISATION; MEDITATIONS; and JOURNEYING — A WAY OF SELF-DISCOVERY... unleashing between them vast possibilities which few of us have ever bothered to even begin to *look at, let alone ex*plore... or enjoy...

Only by reading them will you perceive this to be true; in fact you may find what you read here not only informative and inspiring, but somewhat galvanising — particularly certain sections...

This is what these books are about:

THE POWER OF CREATIVE VISUALISATION is designed to help you master the skill of visualising something, and then *precipitate* it — and this directly or indirectly. However, above all else, it is about *connecting* oneself with the Spirit; and yet it is also of practical import, as you will see...

Whereas MEDITATIONS is an all-out effort to present the art of meditation as a multi-fold experience — which can *unlock* perceptual states of which most people know practically nothing; nevertheless, it is not especially about meditation as practised in the East, be it in India or in Tibet; it is Western Meditation, based on Nature, and on a view of the Cosmos which brings home the full beauty of the Spirit.

Finally there is JOURNEYING — A WAY OF SELF-DISCOVERY. This book was founded on a number of journeys as practised by several groups of people, projecting their consciousness under guidance to various targets around the Solar System and beyond... Alpha Centauri, Sirius, the Pleiades, the centre of the galaxy, and to a planet in the Andromeda galaxy. Intrigued?!

You will find this combined book something of a piece o*f Light,* standing on your nearest bookshelf, and reminding you always of your incredible potential as a human being — a being

1

who can master the art and power of mind and consciousness.

And climb the Cosmic Mountain!

Literally.

NOTES

Where pertinent, the *androgynous* pronouns *s/he* and *hir* (pronounced *her*) have been used when implying both sexes, or either sex. It may take you a little while to get fully used to these, nevertheless the use of these pronouns is infinitely more preferable than using ubiquitous male pronouns for the same purpose.

The pronoun *s-he* is used specifically to imply an androgynous or hermaphroditic being.

The word Spiritu*al* has been capitalised throughout this manual in order to distinguish it from its ordinary religious overtones, or from spiritism or spiritualism. Here it is associated with the word *Spirit,* or that which is formless power.

Capitalised words are used for emphasis, as are all words or phrases set in italics — particularly those which need to be differentiated in meaning from their normal written or spoken equivalents.

Certain Sanskrit words have also be used, wherever possible sparingly, and these are clearly explained during the course of this manual; wherever possible a Western, English word or definition has been used as a substitute.

Occasionally certain abbreviations have been used, in context — such as physical for the physical *body* or the *physical plane*, thus avoiding the overuse of certain words which might make your reading unnecessarily tedious.

In every other respect the writing has been kept simple, despite some of the difficulties of explaining non-physical phenomena when using a language, such as ordinary English, which was designed or else was evolved in order to define ordinary physical events and reality.

This manual forms a part of a series of manuals, which are published by Skoob Books Publishing Ltd. in collaboration with Spiral Publications.

FOREWORD

THE POWER OF CREATIVE VISUALISATION is in many ways different from other books bearing similar titles, for it looks at both the mundane and the esoteric aspects of creative visualisation, and shows how these two are interrelated.

The first three Chapters are concerned predominantly with the mundane side of things; nevertheless they are interlaced with esoteric information which is of direct relevance with regard to acquiring a greater ability to project thought-forms and actualise them to one's own consciousness, then to *precipitate* them into the physical world, directly or indirectly.

It is not suggested that any of this is easy; nor is it particularly complex. The exercises given are written simply, and rather than confound anyone with unusually obscure techniques, those which are essential are represented here, without ambiguity.

In itself, this book is perfectly self-contained. However, you will also find references in brackets to the other SPIRAL PUBLICATIONS/SKOOB BOOKS — these contain additional information which can be usefully merged with that to be found in this book.

In Chapters 4 and 5 you will find information of an esoteric nature. This will permit you to consider the greater implications of creativity in a more Cosmic context, while relating this to the human state.

All in all you should find THE POWER OF CREATIVE VISUALISATION invaluable; it represents the very techniques which have sponsored the birth and unfoldment of SPIRAL PUBLICATIONS, and which are used every day in the attempt to bring you this information.

It is hoped that it will inspire you, and that you will derive much benefit from using and applying it in your own work and life.

SPIRAL PUBLICATIONS — Glastonbury, January 1987.

CHAPTER 1 — YOUR CREATIVE POTENTIAL

1 — ARE YOU CREATIVE?

Inherently the answer, without doubt, is *YES!* — somewhere within you there is a creative spark, and that spark can become a flame; then a fire.

TO BE CREATIVE, ABOVE ALL ELSE, IS TO BE ALIVE!; to feel animated with positive energies which require creative expression — in any one of thousands of different ways, accordingly to your affinities and inclination.

You may already know yourself to be creative, but you may be looking for ways of applying yourself, or for methods of improving your creativity, or simply for inspiration. Or you may not think of yourself as creative, and you are seeking information which may help you to become ALIVE!

Either way you should find this book helpful, as it goes beyond the usual boundaries which attempt to define creativity, and how it works.

Like a magnet, like attracts like. If you are positive towards life, life will become positive towards you; the more you are creative with your life, the more you will find things happening for you, and coming towards you — helpful, challenging, and fulfilling things. From then on you will only want to look forwards.

This book examines several methods of unfolding your creativity, and also ways of perceiving this within a mundane and esoteric context.

2 — SIMPLE VISUALISATION TECHNIQUES

Look at an object around you — for several minutes. Note its form; its colour; its texture. Look at all the details with meticulous attention.

Do not just look at it — try and touch it with your mind. What would it feel like in your hands? Warm, cold, abrasive, sensual, smooth, flexible, solid, hollow, soft, heavy, light?...

What is your subjective response to it? What does it conjure up by way of personal experiences? Does it *feel* good to you? Pleasurable? Indifferent? Not so good?

Play around with these objective and subjective sensations or feelings — and note them down. Then try another object: try about twelve to twenty in all to begin with.

Now draw on a sheet of paper and/or cut out a circle; a line; a triangle; a square; a five-pointed star; an oval; a spiral. Try filling them with different colours. Meditate on each shape: what do these *feel* like to you? What images or situations do they invoke for you? Note these down too.

Go out in nature. Look at the trees, the fields, the sky, the clouds, the Sun (just glance at it very quickly: don't stare at it, obviously) — *feel* them. What do you experience from them? Look at other life-forms around you: birds, animals, plants, flowers, insects... What do they *feel* like to you?

Now do all these things again; this time look not so much at the forms of these objects, but at their energies — *see* each one as energy in form. Note that while each energy is different in its quality and characteristics, it is also the same energy. The same life-force. Further note that all the energy around them is also an expression of the same life-force.

See the ocean of energy which surrounds you.

It is all mind-stuff, expressing life through an infinity of forms.

This is the life-stuff which you will be using in your creativity.

Now close your eyes, and try and see each object in your mind's eye. Try this until you succeed — if you find it difficult at first, do all the first part of these exercises again, then close your eyes once more; and do this until you can see each object clearly and with ease.

Next listen to different sounds. Listen to each one, then to all the sounds you can hear — feel the *sound-scape* around you; do this in different places. Sense how each sound is distinct, how each one conjures up its own reality; and yet how all of them together conjure up a greater ambient reality.

The more you do this, the more you will find it easy to visualise things, because each time you think of them you will conjure up their images, their qualities, their *feel*... They will become part of your conscious experience (quite often what you see and hear around you is perceived only at a semi-conscious to semi-subconscious, and sometimes entirely subconscious level).

The more you can hold an image in your mind, the more you can re-create it in some way, or represent it — directly to indirectly; objectively to subjectively.

Remember to remember (!) the *ocean of energy* — you will be creating things out of it. Each effort that you make to do so, you will be drawing on this life-energy and giving it form.

This is called *materialising* or *precipitating* an object(s); by way of analogy it is very much like vapour — when water (representing the *ocean of energy*) becomes heated by the Sun (representing the *essence* or *power* of Life), it evaporates; as it comes into contact with colder layers of air (representing mind), it becomes clouds (the beginning of the activity of the mind); as the clouds get thicker and more tangible the molecules of vaporised water come closer together — eventually droplets of water are formed, and it rains (condensation = precipitation); if it becomes cold enough it will hail or snow (a greater degree of crystallisation = manifestation).

Now think about this process — how the interplay of hot (Sun/Spirit) and cold (mind) brings about changes in energy states.

When you reach towards the Spirit, things dematerialise. When you condense energy, it becomes precipitated, and it materialises.

Nevertheless a *cold* mind is a *dead* mind; it has to be *animated* by the *heat* of the Spirit. Only then can you direct your creativity at will.

And it needs *heart* — the soul within you — which will put you in contact with all life, and give your mind *magnetic* warmth and power.

THE POWER OF CREATIVE VISUALISATION is designed to maximise your life and your creativity; to help you to draw the things you really want or need towards you; to materialise them for yourself (and maybe for others should you feel inclined to benefit others as well as yourself). It may well change your life in a way that you will welcome and find intensely pleasurable.

It also seeks to put you in touch with your soul and Spirit, for without these creativity is hollow and meaningless; it doesn't resonate in affinity with anything else. It should be said that this is not a matter of religion, as religion is commonly understood, but a matter of acknowledging the fullness of one's life.

Oddly enough the creative process is inherently simplicity itself, once one realises the above and makes it part of one's life at a conscious level. Nevertheless, we live in a dense environment on a day to day basis, and to precipitate something on a physical level into our lifes requires some effort.

On the Mental Plane, one can just think of something, and it is there. On the physical plane, one has to build up the image on the Mental Place first, bring it down through the Astral Plane (representing feelings), and then materialise it objectively on that physical plane — directly, or indirectly.

At present you may not be familiar with the idea of a Mental Plane and an Astral Plane — unless you have read the other books in this series, or other books which describe these. For now just try and picture to yourself a Cosmos which has many different levels of existence, all superimposed within the same space, and that you are a being who has many different sides — that is, there is more to you than merely a physical, biological body.

There are stories of Adepts who can materialise an object in the palms of their hands, or at a distance. Most of us are not likely to be quite that talented. Yet you can manifest things for yourself in much the same way, by visualising them, attracting them, and then precipitating them into your life — the process may be less direct, yet intrinsically it will be similar.

In fact your imagination is your only limit. Conversely, you will find it difficult to precipitate something which is *too big* for you to handle; try simple things to begin with. This, of course, makes sense nevertheless there are always those who will try and manifest something which is way beyond their ken or ability to precipitate, and then they may become despondent because the *system* doesn't work for them.

As you begin to feel more confident about the causes and the effects of your efforts, you will find it easier to manifest *bigger* things.

Creativity is an evolutionary exercise. Nature — as we see it around us — was not built in a day! It all happened bit by bit — one experiment leading to a result, leading in turn towards another experiment and another result. Nature learnt from these results: she took what was useful, and rejected what was not. She adapted her creations to the needs of the time; and she stored away information which might prove to be of relevance later.

Nature is not *blind*, like some care to think she is (they say this because *they* are the ones who are blind!).

She builds herself out of the energy which she is; she evolves out of need, and in response to the life within the forms.

As you feel more able within yourself to be fully creative you can *expand* in leaps and bounds — visualising what you can do, *feeling* it, and materialising it...

3 — THE USE OF MEDITATION

Meditation is a way of *aligning* yourself with the object or subject of your meditation. In this way you are creating a direct, conscious path between you and it; it gives you access to this object or subject. You can move your consciousness from one point to another, and in this way tune your consciousness into a great number of different possibilities, or actualities at some level or another.

Visualisation is a type of meditation — not only do you create that path, or bridge, you also access the possibility and actuality of *manipulating* your own mind ... which is infinitely better than allowing anyone or anything else to manipulate it for you. You can learn to visualise things the way that you want to manifest them. You can become conscious of the creative potential which you have: you can learn to express that inherent creativity; and if you apply yourself in the right way you will get results.

Nevertheless it always requires at least some effort — it doesn't just happen without input on your part.

Meditation in itself can be a source of endless inspiration (in MEDITATION, a sister book to this one, you will find much by way of information which you will find of direct usefulness in this context). Above all else, meditation can permit you to *link up* with the more subjective parts of your nature in order to perceive Life in a way that will give wings to your creativity.

Inspiration for many people is a fickle affair: it comes and it goes, and it doesn't always come when it seems to be needed. Learning to be creative with your life means that it will come to you more readily when it is needed.

... The more you flow with that inspiration, the more it will come to you — more and more effortlessly. But the effort to materialise your intent will still be needed.

Therefore meditating regularly — as an intrinsic part of your life, and not just as an occasional *add-on* - will make many things possible which you may have thought were impossible, or perhaps only unlikely. Your work can be a meditation as well; meditation is not confined to moments of silence.

4 — THE NATURAL WAY

Nature is everywhere around you, and within you. To live naturally is to acknowledge this, and to flow with Nature.

There are those who care to drive a conceptual wedge between Spirit and Nature, yet the Spirit can be seen as:

(1) a higher octave of Nature

(2) the Essence of Nature.

And Nature as the manifestation of the Spirit.

When the two are seen as two aspects of the same One Life, there is no longer any meaningful division between them. In their aspected configuration they are co-creative elements within a Whole.

As we noted earlier, the third aspect is the *Heart* — the mediator between Spirit and Nature; the Soul. And to be truly creative requires soulfulness.

But what does that mean or entail?

The Soul-element within us is that part of us which directs the personality lives that we lead from incarnation to incarnation. It accumulates all the experiences that we have, and learns from the results of incarnation. Therefore, from one angle, it is a vast storehouse of information and experience — and we can draw whatever we need from this reservoir.

All of us know a lot more than we seem to know consciously — because we have accumulated a lot of knowledge and abilities in the past, including in other lives. Learning to *connect* with the information and experience in this store-house makes creativity all the more possible — because we have all been creative in that past, in some manner or other. Within the greater store-house of the collective Soul there is even more information and experience, and this can be drawn upon as well.

As we have seen, the Heart is also magnetic in character. The Spirit represents power; Nature represents the manifestation of that power: the Soul represents that which handles the power, funnels it, and disseminates it into manifestation.

The Animistic view is that all of Nature is alive with Soul; everything which exists is inherently soulful — even so-called inanimate objects and substances.

Try the following exercise:

Concentrate on your heart chakra (the power-point within the left ventricle of the heart, which projects itself somewhere in the region of your sternum), and imagine yourself to be a magnet; imagine yourself to be drawing your conscious personality into affinity, then alignment, and finally into fusion with your Soul-self; and then from that vantage, to be drawing your needs towards you — whatever these needs may be.

Feel currents of magnetic attraction stretching out into the space around you, seeking out those needs, connecting with them, and then these needs being drawn towards you. Do this every day — at first this may seem too subjective to be real, or particularly effective. Later you will realise that it works! Quite naturally.

To the extent that you motivate yourself with will, with heart and with intelligence, these needs will come to you — in some form or another, and sooner or later.

5 — IDEAS

As far as creativity goes, ideas are crucial. They are the life and blood of any creative effort. Without them, creativity is impossible.

Most people have ideas; yet few people put them into action. Those who have few ideas live relatively unfruitful lives: those who have ideas, but do not exercise them creatively, fare little better.

At the other end of the spectrum, some people have lots of ideas, but cannot find the time or the inclination to materialise them all — they usually select those which they feel they can deal with within the context of their lives, and take whatever steps are necessary in order to make them work for themselves.

However, not all ideas are right; some can be destructive or harmful; or indifferent; or inappropriate. Ideas can also lead to ideals, which in turn can lead to dogma — and dogma is never right in itself either — regardless of what it is based on; and regardless of who may have promoted the ideas in the first place.

One can share an idea, or ideas, in a variety of ways — one can write about them; one can create something which expresses those ideas; or one can infer an idea through the medium of another form of expression.

In practical terms one can use ideas not only creatively, but in business — in fact a business without ideas is either a dying business, or one which relies on a hoo*k* something which creates a craving, for instance.

You have probably heard of the expression of "an idea whose time has come" — i.e., the expression of that idea will inspire people because they have reached the stage when they can be readily receptive to it; because they need it.

All businesses and movements which are not only out to survive, but also to grow and expand, must be capable of generating ideas which are needed.

What do you need? What ideas can you generate for yourself?

Imagine yourself to be surrounded by an infinite space (which is a fact; you are!). Within that infinite space there are an infinite number of beings expressing an infinite number of ideas.

Narrow down the focus of your inner lens; presently around you, on this planet, there are approximately between four and five billion people in incarnation; and there are many more who are not in incarnation, yet who are still very much attached to the evolution and life of this planet. Out of these four to five billion *incarnates* there is a significant fraction of people who are capable of either *channelling* an idea, or ideas, or of generating one.

This idea is not necessarily theirs, in the pure sense at least — they may have *picked it up* from someone else, because as soon as someone thinks of an idea it generates a thought-form, which then *floats* around until it disintegrates from lack of attention; ideas also come into existence because they are the end results of other idea-processes; and whenever there is a genuine group need, then appropriate ideas will find form anyway — quite naturally — either through one person, or else through a whole number of people all more or less simultaneously.

Which explains why different people in different parts of the world occasionally have the same idea at the same time; and why resultant issues of copyright can be very difficult to judge in some circumstances.

And it also explains why certain ideas reoccur from age to age — whenever they are needed. Some of these could be categorised as *archetypal ideas*. Others are just good ideas which are applicable in different cultural settings.

Getting back to stories about Adepts, it is said that certain *Masters* spend at least some of their valuable time just generating ideas for other people to pick up on; those who are most likely to be able to *channel* those ideas will do so, or may do so.

6 — THE UNFOLDMENT OF IDEAS

An idea on its own is not usually up to much. If it is not *earthed* or *grounded* in the right sort of way, it just remains an idea, therefore remains unused. Even if it is precipitated into tangible existence it may not attract any interest — either because it is not communicated in such a way that the attention of others will be stimulated; or because other ideas have arisen which people may find more compelling at the time.

An example of this is the case of compact discs — when these were first promoted a few years ago another system was being evolved which was far superior; it was cheaper; it was more flexible; and it was potentially much easier to produce.

Instead of a disc, there was a card, and this could be reproduced by lithographic means. On this card could be found digital information in printed form. The system required a *reading* device, which like the systems using compact discs, was based around a laser. The company which had devised it struggled — as it turned out in vain — to beat the compact disc systems into the market place.

The idea was better, but too many companies had already paid allegiance to the idea of compact discs, and had invested considerable resources in that direction; and, of course, they wanted a return on that investment. The alternative, ultimately more cost-effective system, was ignored.

The world is full of these examples. IBM set a world standard with its PC range of computers, which though relatively mediocre, was the first standard to emerge from out of the plethora of incompatible computer systems. To the despair of many computer buffs it is now the case that dozens of companies are energetically competing with each other to produce cheaper and/or better, and/or faster, yet basically outdated, PC clones — even though there are computers and operating systems which are far more advanced and far more interesting than the standard set by IBM.

If one idea leads to another, it is not always a certainty that the latest or even the best idea will *catch on*, because companies which can afford to *push* their products tend to win out against their competitors, even if these have better ideas and better products.

You might well think that this applies only to business; it doesn't! It applies to art; it applies to religion; it applies to philosophy; it applies to science; it applies to politics; and it even applies to esoteric knowledge.

Does this serve the best interest of humanity? The answer, strangely enough, is yes and no — because it forces people to come up with even better and more flexible ideas. It forces them to be more organised, and to use their intelligence to the limit. Nevertheless many good ideas will still be lost or neglected.

If we lived in an *ideal* society, it would be fair to expect that whatever was better would be adopted. In our sort of world it is not what is best which is adopted, but what is expediently marketable.

Against this we have the many shining examples of the humble making good. Going back to computers, as an example, Apple started in a private garage with practically no funds whatsoever (Apple's originators sold an old WV in order to raise their initial finances). Today Apple is a big, and ever-growing business.

Anyone with enough determination can rise above circumstances, and make hirself heard — one way or the other.

Nevertheless, if one is to succeed one must *string together* ideas in a viable sequence — one idea may well lead to another, but it must also lead to the *right* sort of idea — one which will work within the framework that one is considering or enacting, and one which will work within the framework of the outside world — keeping in mind that things are forever changing.

Mould-busting ideas may surface in one's mind, yet they have to be applied with a lot of care and due attention before they are likely to upset the status quo. In business, in particular, one must have more than just good ideas; one must have intelligence, intuition, and will. One must be able to produce goods in sufficient quantities at a price which will be attractive to potential customers; one must be able to promote these goods through clever (and preferably honest) advertising, addressed to people through the most appropriate channels within one's means; one must have a good public relations department; one must be able to organise one's business to cater for delays, set-backs, and events beyond one's immediate control; one must be organised about one's finances, to the extent that over-reaching in one's expenses does not grossly exceed one's income; one must be able to provide a good service to one's customers, which will mean that those customers will come back for more; one must innovate and consolidate as a matter of form and principle; one must encourage oneself and one's co-workers (i.e., staff) to be productive, and provide them with agreeable conditions of work, and attractive salaries; one must look to the future, and identify possible, if not the most likely trends to come; one must manage all one's resources wisely... etc.

This requires not only mental prowess — it requires extraordinary skills in many departments. It is perhaps the bane of our existing society that we rely on competition rather than on global co-operation to secure a *positive* result.

Will the New Age change this? This depends on us — those of us who are sufficiently motivated to change things towards something better.

Those who complain that things are wrong, yet are not prepared to initiate something better, are not doing themselves, or anyone else, any service at all. Things do not change because of complaints alone; they change only because enough people *make* it change by being sufficiently organised in what they do, and by applying the right amount of effort and ideas to whatever problems may exist. Again, this requires will, determination, intuition and intelligence — and not so much revolution as it does creative, dynamic evolution.

Therefore being creative generally means much more than just expressing one's individual inventiveness; if it cannot be applied to the life that we live in a way which changes things towards what we need and want, it is as good as naught.

The unfoldment of ideas is a structural phenomenon, and yet one may occasionally witness *quantum jumps* occurring, caused by lateral movements of mind and intuition. These can cause things to accelerate, and sometimes change radically — often with unpredictable results. In order to make sure that these *jumps* become useful they must be integrated into the overall changes we are seeking — which means one must continually remain alert to any and all these changes; and then one must act accordingly, and intelligently — and with flexibility.

Whatever our visions of the future may be, wherever our affinities may lie, we are an integral part of the planetary human and ecological life which surrounds us. Information now reaches us from all parts of the globe. That information — however partial it may be on occasions — gives us *tools* to work with. Excesses can be countered creatively, rather than destructively; what is really useful can be enhanced; people's views can be encouraged to change whenever they are at odds with planetary needs.

Taking this into account it is often better to be unitive in one's approach, rather than creating divisions between people. Regardless of those forces in play which may not appeal to us, it is far better to be creative than it is to fight against an opposition — which need not be perceived as an opposition; unless it is seen as an unconscious factor which is there to spur us on towards a better definition of our efforts.

The old tests the new; that, in the final analysis, may be its saving grace. It does fulfil a useful function in that respect.

7 — GIVING POWER TO YOUR IDEAS

If in the last section we have ventured into considering matters which may be interpreted as surpassing any personal needs with regard to creativity, it must be pointed out that creativity always occurs within a cultural context.

An idea in itself has power, yet as soon as it is relinquished from consciousness much, if not all of that power tends to vanish.

If you have good ideas — which you intend using — you will need to give them additional power; how can one do this?

Meditating on each idea, or set of ideas, is one way. Meditation will help you to define those ideas further; it will add energy to your thought-forms, and it will encourage associated ideas to emerge into your consciousness.

Using your mind you can then manipulate those ideas, make alterations, and *test* them for their integrity and usefulness.

Let us say that you want to build something — for instance, a hand loom. Your problem is that you know how conventional looms are made, but it takes too long to set up the warp on traditional designs — perhaps 45 minutes even for a simple 2-inch wide belt.

You know how long you want your belts to be — therefore your warp length needs to be of that length, plus a bit extra to allow for the end section which cannot be woven. Traditionally, hand looms use a system of heddle bars and wire heddles — which means that each warp line must pass through one heddle loop; then each warp line must be passed through one of the divisions in a metal screen or comb which acts as a weft beater. Since the loom frame is fixed it means that each warp line must be inserted separately, and then groups of warp lines must be adjusted for tension — using a tie bar.

What you want is a loom where you can lay on the warp very quickly, without fiddling with heddles or a weft comb-beater.

Therefore you may begin to meditate on a rough idea you have had for a continuous warp frame.

The next problem is that you still have to pass your wool (or other warp materials) around the warp frame; this takes less time than it does on a conventional design, but it still takes too long.

During your meditation you come up with a design which incorporates a revolving warp frame within an outer loom frame — this would permit you to tie on the first warp line, say to the left of the warp frame, revolve the warp frame through 360 degrees (placing that warp line in a notch at the other end of the warp frame as you go), and then access the departure point again for the second warp line, etc. As you come back to the front of the warp frame you can tie on another warp line of a different colour to the previous warp line; by building up your colours you will be able to get colour patterns.

So far so good. But how do you make the whole design solid enough to take the impact of the weaving process?

The outer frame must be rock solid; and the warp frame must be able to revolve easily. As you meditate you calculate the effect of stress bars added to the outer loom frame in order to make it solid enough; you further calculate the gaps which are necessary to make sure that the warp frame will not collide with or scrape against the outer frame. Finally you see how to make feet for the loom which will keep the outer frame upright.

Final touches to your creative visualisation/meditation include a warp tension bar, simple heddle bars with toggles, and string heddles; a number of bolts and screws; and a weft stick, which doubles up as a weft beater.

(I've used this example, because a few years ago I was recovering from a road accident, and I couldn't walk very far without suffering the consequences. I wanted to work, but I couldn't get around very easily, so it had to be something that I could do at home. I'd worked with looms before, and come against the frustrations of setting these up for weaving. It took me eight hours of continuous meditation to *design* the sort of loom described above, checking each detail in my mind as to whether it would work or not. When I was finally convinced that it would work, I committed the idea to paper, then I bought some wood, and I made it; and it worked perfectly. I could put on a 28-line multi-coloured warp in less than four minutes — which was a great improvement on traditional designs. To this day I have never come across another loom quite like it. More importantly, this process taught me how to meditate on an idea which was designed to be practical in its application, as distinct from using meditation to explore purely subjective or Spiritual states. Therefore, starting with a rough idea, and then using creative visualisation/meditation, a complete and workable design was evolved — integral, without any recourse to pen and paper, except after I had finished the meditation. This was a relatively simple idea — with a measure of design difficulty nevertheless. The idea was given power — by meditating on it intensely — and a complete and detailed thought-form was generated. All that was needed next was to precipitate it by building it.)

Giving your ideas power means meditating on them in gradually more and more detail, until the result you need is achieved. When finally you can see that result in your mind's eye, and when you can hold it there, unwaveringly, your thought-form then has power.

You can add extra power, by deliberately breathing light into it and by increasing your ability to channel power (see MEDITATIONS).

CHAPTER 2 — CREATIVE VISUALISATION

8 — THE ACT OF SEEING

Seeing what is around us is very much a factor of how we have been conditioned to see them; unless blind, we all have eyes which perceive the diffracted reflections of light off the objects we look at, yet *what* we see depends to a great degree on cultural consensus.

Here are two quick examples to illustrate this: (1) nearly 500 years ago when the Spaniards anchored their ships off the coast of what is now Mexico, the local indians could not see these ships (at first) — because these had shapes which were outside of their cultural norms. But they saw the Spaniards, because according to their legends, and their chronological, cyclical prophecies, they were in fact expecting the *white gods* to return on that particular day, and the Spaniards happened to be white (or at least whiter that they were); (2) many people who have seen a UFO event in common, at the same time and place, report having seen different things — a technological flying craft; globules of light; an angel; or maybe some saw nothing, whereas others saw *something*; etc. In the 19th century people were seeing exotic air ships instead; over two thousand years ago people were seeing *chariots of fire*. In each case people may have been aware that *something* was there, but they perceived it in different ways according to what made sense to them (or else they did not perceive it at all, as in the case of the indians and the Spaniards' ships).

Therefore there is a difference between seeing, and interpreting what is seen — even at a perceptual level.

Another example: if you talk to a policeman about people's perceptions of any given road accident he may tell you that all the witnesses, when questioned, in effect saw the event of the accident; nevertheless in each case the details of what each person saw were different — and this partly because s/he may have seen the accident from a different position or angle, but also because each witness interpreted what occurred in hir own fashion (which can include hidden or overt prejudices as well).

Secondly, although we see the reflected light from objects around us, each object or creature has its own internal light — its etheric *aura* or energy field, if you like, which is also known as bioplasmic, or bioplasmatic energy. This is not ordinary light, and it cannot normally be seen because it exists in a different range(s) of the electro-magnetic spectrum. Some psychics can see it, however; most people cannot.

Thirdly, some psychics can see light in ranges which are Astral, Mental — i.e., pertaining to those Planes. Advanced Initiates can see into ranges which are Buddhic, Atmic, or even Monadic...

In esoteric terms, whatever is seen that is not physical is perceived with the *third eye*, or ajna chakra — which is an evolutionary development and outgrowth corresponding to the chakras or power-points which are associated with the pineal and pituitary endocrine glands. When awakened, this *third eye* makes itself felt just above the eyeline, in the middle of the forehead.

While initially creative visualisation may be dependent on one's sense of physical or normal sight, true creative visualisation requires the use of this *third eye*, or ajna (which is the Sanskrit word for it).

9 — *PROJECTING THOUGHT-FORMS*

Some people have great difficulty actually visualising objects subjectively — that is, they find it nearly impossible to form a picture of an object in their minds.

Some people are visually oriented; others are verbally oriented.

According to one popular theory with regard to how the brain works, the right cerebral hemisphere is visually oriented, and the left cerebral hemisphere is verbally oriented — even though both hemispheres have visual and verbal receptors. The right part of the brain is *subjective*, and the left part is *objective*, or *illogical-*

intuitive and *logical*; subconscious (and potentially superconscious) and conscious; female and male.

While this theory may be in some ways unsatisfactory, it does draw one's attention to the differentiation between subjective and objective perception.

An example here: during the course of a TV documentary viewers were presented with the case of a man who had a damaged left brain. To illustrate what this could mean in terms of perception, the man was asked to look at a computer VDU screen. This screen had a line running down the middle, and words and images were alternatively presented on the left and the right side of that line. What transpired was that when a word was presented on the left side, the man was incapable of seeing it; yet when asked to relax and draw what might have been there he invariably, and correctly, drew the image equivalent of that word. His right cerebral hemisphere had *filled in* the gap in his perceptions by reproducing the equivalent image corresponding to the word.

If the man had had, instead, a similarly damaged right cerebral hemisphere, it is likely that his left brain would have interpreted an image on the right of the line as a word.

In our culture we (mostly men) pride ourselves somewhat with regard to our sense of *logic* — if something can be explained rationally, then it is likely that it will be accepted as a part of our cultural consensus; whereas things which appear to be *illogical* are often frowned upon, and are usually rejected (particularly if they are truly baffling! — i.e., totally outside of the parameters of our consensus *reality*). As a result men (especially) tend to divide life into two camps, and they only accept perceptions which fit in neatly with their sense of *logic*, in other words in one of those two camps. Women, conversely, and speaking generally, are often more intuitively oriented; they can have perceptions which are seemingly *illogical*, i.e., which do not make rational sense, yet they will tend to accept them as perfectly valid — because their *intuitions* tell them that they are *true*. Equally, and on occasions, they may find logical explanations *untrue*, because, likewise, their *intuitions* tell them that these explanations are *false*.

Going further, and doing a bit of comparative, anthropological research, one comes to realise that what may pass for as *logic* in one culture is dubbed *illogical* in another; and vice-versa. Keeping this in mind one may further realise that matters of *logic* and *illogic* are far more subjective than they may otherwise appear to be at first. One culture may be *left brain oriented*, and another may be *right brain oriented*, and people of different cultures will interpret their perceptions accordingly.

If one was to introduce the notion of several races of extraterrestrials into the picture, it is a fairly safe bet that this would seem compounded to the nth degree!

This is a round-about way of saying that nothing is fixed; one person's idea of what is structurally sound is another person's idea of chaos. Whatever we may undertake in the creative department is likely to be based on what we accept as *real*, subjectively and/or objectively, which does not mean that there are not greater, or different realities to be perceived and known.

Creating thought-forms is in itself an automatic process which is triggered as soon as as we think — especially if we think visually, i.e., if we can picture an object, or a series of objects in our minds.

To take full advantage of this one must train oneself to see mental pictures — first of all by using simple visualisation techniques, if necessary (as related in Chapter 1, Section 2); then by learning to conjure up any mental image at will.

Thirdly, and ideally, one must learn to *see* things psychically — on the Astral and/or Mental Planes; i.e., one can access these levels directly and consciously. Whenever this is achieved one can *see* the projections of one's own thought-forms as *real* — these manifest themselves in astral/mental space as objects which are perfectly tangible, and sometimes vividly so.

This requires practice, but otherwise it does not entail anything particularly far-fetched — however it can be quite stunning when it actually happens, i.e., when one actually and consciously perceives things at that level, or levels. By concentrating all one's attention on a mental image one can become so aware of one's own projections of that image that eventually one *sees* it in much the same way as one would see a physical object although, if anything, it may seem more intense — especially in its colouration and luminosity.

Once this has been done, then the process of materialising it becomes far easier — because it already has a lot of power associated with its potential manifestation.

Try conjuring up any number of different images of objects at will, in your mind's eye, and this in relatively quick succession. You will probably find that some are easier to see than are others, and this is perhaps because you are more familiar with certain objects or shapes than you are with others. Nevertheless, persevere over a period of time, and you will find yourself able to create any image that you like in your mind, and then manipulate it in any way that you want.

Accessing astral and mental space directly does require training (see THE PSYCHIC EXPLORER). That training is useful, because it will give you more control over your visualisations; and should you actually manage to project your consciousness out of your physical body you will also come to appreciate your inherent ability to practise creative visualisation and manifestation or precipitation instantaneously and with minimal effort, at least while fully immersed and conscious in that state — this is not only fun or interesting, it will also bring home to you the validity of everything which has been said so far.

10 — HOLDING THE IMAGE IN YOUR MIND

The next *trick* to learn is to hold an image steady in your mind's eye — for minutes on end, even hours. Again this requires practice, yet it also requires a *giving of power* to the image from your own *power stock*. How can one best explain this process?

By virtue of living we are all the embodiment of a certain amount of power. The greater percentage of people now living do not have all that much personal power; conversely, an Adept or a capable Shaman has a lot of personal power, in relative terms at least; and what is more s/he can draw readily on other sources of power in order to boost hir *stock* and then implement an act.

Assuming that those of us reading this might fall somewhere in between these two extremes, what can we do to increase our quota of personal power?

Meditation is one possibility (see THE PSYCHIC EXPLORER, and MEDITATIONS, which follows this piece). One can learn to draw more power into ourselves in that way. The Carlos Castaneda books give some interesting insights into the shamanic way of doing this; the Alice Bailey books afford some cogent information from a Tibetan esoteric viewpoint also.

Try this exercise: lie down on your bed and look at the ceiling. Then project a mental image of your choice while using your ceiling as a projection screen (this is best done in subdued light conditions incidentally). For purposes of *demonstration* let us say that this image is that of a huge two-dimensional butterfly — with well defined colourations.

Practise this until you can see it clearly.

11 — MANIPULATING THE IMAGE WITH YOUR MIND

So you can see the clear graphic outline of a giant butterfly. Now try manipulating this image in a variety of ways: first, change its colourations, yet without changing anything of its outline. Let us say that it is a blue butterfly, with red spots on its wings, and yellow fringes towards the extremities of its wing tips. Change the blue to orange, the red to green, and the yellow to indigo or violet; then hold that image and its colourations as steadily as you can in your mind. Then try some other colour combinations.

Once you have got this far, try and initiate a continuous wash or roll of colours — i.e., from moment to moment all these colourations are being changed.

Next, give the image a three-dimensional perspective; then make its wings beat and its antennae quiver.

Admittedly, your creative, materialising genius is probably not very intent on precipitating giant butterflies into physical reality (conversely you may become very popular in some circles if you actually succeed!). Now try projecting the image of something that you might need in some way.

As an adjunct to this exercise, visualise yourself associated with that image (for instance, say you need a new typewriter; visualise yourself working on that typewriter; feel the keys beneath your fingers; look at the word on the sheet of paper which is being typed upon).

In this fashion you can experiment with any number of different kinds of needs — nevertheless, it is best to try and manifest only one of these at a time — at least until you are more proficient at materialising anything at all.

When you do these sorts of things you *align* your consciousness and your mind with the object or the subject of your needs — it is not easy to actually precipitate an object into physical reality just by visualising it, and presto, there it is standing in front of you! What does happen, however, is that you broadcast your intent and your needs on the ethers, and somehow you draw the physical reality of that object towards you. It may come to you in any number of different ways, and through any number of possible sources — yet sooner or later it will come, and often when you are not expecting it as well.

The time it takes to precipitate an object varies according to the amount of power that you may give to your visualisations. Most of us, if we are truly honest, are pretty lazy; therefore if we do a visualisation once or twice, and think that this effort is enough, well it is usually not enough, and the object will not appear, directly, or indirectly. Nevertheless if we keep visualising the object of our intent, over whatever period of time may be necessary, then it will most certainly come towards us, or manifest itself... providing we are not blocking it from doing so in other ways — for instance, by having doubts that it will come towards us; or because of any subconscious rejection of it, including not feeling worthy of it, etc.

Likewise, if you want to heal yourself of a bruised leg, or even a broken bone, for example, imagine this leg or bone as being perfectly healthy — and full of light, or life-force. If on the other hand one keeps thinking of this leg or bone as bruised or broken, then this hinders the healing process.

If your needs are more subjective, then you may have to rely on symbolic associations. Say you need a piece of information, but that you do not know where to find it. Imagine yourself going up to a bookshelf, opening a book which you feel will contain that information, and then reading that information from its pages. If you cannot actually read the words, do not worry. Providing you have put enough energy into your visualisation you will find that this information will become available to you over the next few days — it may not necessarily come in the form of a book, however.

In order to implement the full power of creative visualisation it is also useful to learn how to reach an *in-between* state of consciousness — that is, in-between physical and astral. Similar exercises to those used for projecting out of the body can be initiated: relaxing fully; achieving the *floating state* (again refer to THE PSYCHIC EXPLORER); then doing the visualisation. The results can be spectacular, in as much as one can retain full control over the degree of consciousness one imparts to both the the physical and astral levels. As one *shifts* one's attention into the astral state of awareness, one's consciousness becomes fully *astralised* — and then one sees the object of one's visualisation perfectly clearly. Or one can start the visualisation, then gradually *shift* one's attention into an astralised state, while maintaining the visualisation throughout; or one can do this, and gradually and consciously enter into a dream state, and then have full conscious control over this dream — which is of one's own making. i.e., it is a deliberate projection on one's part. The same can be done with music, until one hears the sounds quite audibly and with absolute realism — in this manner, and within your head, you can learn to keep several instruments all going at once, including percussion sounds, and all of these effortlessly synchronised with a particular rhythm of your own choice. It's great fun doing this, and it is a perfect demonstration of the creative mind at work.

There are those who will say that experiences of this kind are all imaginary; that they are not *real*. However, when dealing with *mind space* anything can be interpreted as being both *real* as well as illusionary — it is quite true that these are instances of the imagination at work; and, yes, these are projections of the mind, and nothing else but that. Nevertheless what counts here is how *real* one can make these seem to oneself — then one can derive useful abilities and information from these projections. From an experiential angle these experiences do have their own aura of reality, yet they remain projections, therefore one can also say that they are illusionary.

It is all a matter of interpretation.

One can even touch an object one has thus visualised and created, and it will feel *real* to the touch — in exactly the same way as a similar physical object would feel *real*.

The mind is capable of astonishing things, and once one accepts this, then the boundaries of one's perceptions and experience can be extended in any number of different ways.

For instance, one can be hypnotised into a trance state, and then be told that one is going to experience six months of training in a given area of creativity — let us say in some artistic field. One can then experience a continuous period of subjective time which appears to last for six months, during which period one is trained, say by a teacher, to do excellent artwork — even though the trance itself will only last perhaps ten minutes of physical clock time.

This is exactly what happened to a young woman in New York — she was hypnotised into a trance state, and when she re-emerged from that trance state she could give an account — detail by detail — of her six months of training and life in this supposedly entirely subjective state. In effect, ten *physical* minutes later she was able to produce artwork which was vastly superior, as well as more inspired, and more inspiring, than anything else she had ever done before, technically and otherwise.

What is more important? Taking advantage of these possibilities, or else arguing about the relative *reality* or illusionary nature of the experience?

You can also try and communicate with your subconscious mind — it is not really the purpose of this book to delve into this possibility at any length, but you can manifest your needs by asking your subconscious mind to make them available to you. This is best done in meditation, or just before going to sleep — although you may have to do this repeatedly before it works for you.

Your subconscious will then exercise its own power, and do whatever you request of it — providing you address it as a friend, clearly and without ambiguity, and providing you do not ask it to manifest unreasonably difficult things, or try and coerce it in any fashion. If you want to try this you should either phrase your request, or visualise it, in very simple terms; if you are too complex about it your subconscious will probably, (1) do nothing at all; (2) manifest the wrong thing, subject to its own interpretation of what you have asked for; (3) present you with a completely inadequate response.

Communicate with your subconscious mind as if it were a young child; do not confuse it with elaborate demands just be clear and simple about these.

12 — HEARING THE SOUNDS

This section is only added here for those who might wish to incorporate more esoteric notions into their creative visualisations.

Each colour, each shape, and each level of energy, has its own sound. Try and hear the sound(s) of an image which you have projected. If you can do so, and you will probably have to practise this at some length before you can manage this, then fully integrate the image with the sound(s) — in your mind and consciousness. Each time you do this visualisation, reinforce this integration — by projecting both the image and the sound(s). Then every time you visualise the image, you will hear its sound(s); or every time you hear or reproduce the sound(s) in your mind, you will see the image. Sooner or later you will find that this is immeasurably useful with regard to the act of precipitating an object.

Likewise the same can be done with regard to accessing a higher state of consciousness. There are certain sounds which when uttered can help *lift* or elevate one's consciousness into various *inner* perceptual states, and which can therefore permit one to become conscious of the *Spirit within*.

Which represents a different order of *Reality*, it should be noted.

The word or mantra, "OM", for instance, when uttered so as to consciously access one's Higher, or Spiritual Self, and the level of consciousness and perceptions which are associated with that Higher Self, can induce a *shift* of one's attention — and thus one can become consciously aware of various *inner-world* perspectives, from which in turn one may derive many insights of great interest to oneself... including information and perceptions which can be directly useful with regard to the act of creating and precipitating objects, or else which may be simply very inspiring — and inspiration is one of the *tools* which any creator, or creatrix, will need.

This mantra needs to be voiced in such a way that it resonates throughout one's whole being — i.e., so that it will make each cell of one's body vibrate to its sound, and so that all one's other energies, including non-physical energies, will also vibrate in resonance to this mantra. Finding the right pitch which will work best for oneself is a matter of experimenting with different frequencies.

...Or of *hearing* the sounds which are emitted by one's chakras, particularly the parachakras above one's head, which are situated in the higher part of one's energy field, or aura.

CHAPTER 3 — GETTING ORGANISED

13 — FEET ON THE EARTH

One of the effects of travelling on a mystical path is that one's consciousness tends to become increasingly abstracted, and therefore one's interest in the mundane world becomes gradually less and less pronounced. The deficit of this effect is that one can become very impractical, to the extent that one fails to experiment with the more creative possibilities afforded by worldly living.

Ideally there needs to be a balance — an ability to explore the Higher Planes, while also exploring one's potential on the physical plane; better yet, one needs to synchronise both activities, and see and live them as a whole, rather than considering these as two separate parts in one's life.

Whatever we do by way of creative work on the physical plane can be seen as a preparation for future creative work on the Higher Planes (at this point we are going to have a look at some of the more esoteric possibilities with regard to creative visualisation); and from another point of view, whatever we do that is creative while incarnate is occurring *concurrently* with whatever it is that we are doing on other levels of existence from the vantage point of our Higher Selves.

It may take you a little while to fully understand what this statement actually implies — from one angle, it is simple; from another, it hints at a sort of *parallelism* which you may not have considered before.

One could argue that to materialise our creative efforts is to *draw down the energies of the Spirit* into the mundane world, thereby helping the physical plane to become somewhat more *Spiritualised* and dynamic. Doing this much not only improves the quality of our personal lives, but it also affects everything around us in a positive manner.

To do this we have to be eminently practical, as well as

inspired. We need to be able to abstract our consciousness, and then return from that state at will. This requires a lot of personal flexibility.

In the Carlos Castaneda books this is described as *stalking*; the ability to be very precise about what one is doing, on this plane, or on any other level. It represents a complete control of one's consciousness, and therefore of one's energy output — in other words it is the best way of dealing with any given situation, because one wastes absolutely *nothing* of one's energy.

There is much more to *stalking* than this, but this is one way of describing what it consists of as an *act* (read THE POWER OF SILENCE, Castaneda).

Conversely, *dreaming* is to abstract one's consciousness from the physical or mundane level (during astral projection, for instance). In effect what one sees and experiences replaces what one sees and experiences normally, which is therefore obscured for a while.

The *Spiritual warrior*, or *Spiritual explorer*, needs to excel in both the arts of *stalking* and *dreaming*. This balance is vital. If that balance does not exist, then certain possibilities and opportunities will be missed — which in the shaman's world is bad news indeed. In a figurative manner of speech it is like trying to drive a car without wheels; or possessing the wheels, but having no car! Or having both, but being unable to drive, or go anywhere — in other words it is unproductive, and potentially dangerous.

The question has always been, if one is *going for the Spirit* — i.e., putting all one's efforts into accessing the inner worlds — how does one go about putting an equal amount of energy into remaining *earthed?* How does one keep one's feet on the ground?

Or conversely, how does one remain normal, as well as do all sorts of things which are totally unearthly?

Again, this is where the art of the *stalker* comes in useful — because s/he learns to perceive what hir true needs actually are, and how to *actuate* them, and therefore s/he will also learn to do whatever is necessary in this respect. S/he uses hir will to remain *grounded*, when s/he needs to *earthed*; and s/he uses hir will when s/he needs to *fly*, or access the inner spaces, or whatever.

Someone who is very practical may or may not be very Spiritually oriented — however, if s/he is not then s/he is unlikely to do anything which will inspire others very much, or even hirself; therefore it is also necessary to consider the Spiritual angle of life in order to *activate* the true benefits of creative visualisation.

Ultimately everyone has to face the *immeasurable beyond*, and therefore, at that time, must make a choice as to which direction s/he is going to go in, and how s/he is going to apply hir energies in consequence.

Nevertheless the whole point of this manual is to provide information on how to change the world we are living in while incarnate, and this creatively.

Therefore let us get on with this consideration.

14 — THE VITAL EXPERIMENT

Is your life a vital experiment, of intense interest to yourself? Do you feel that you are learning from everything which you do? Do you feel *charged up* by both the *doing* and the results of your *doing*?

It is very easy to become complacent and to ignore the possibilities afforded by one's potential.

Whenever the answer is *No*, then you need to remember that you can do something about it, at any time; regardless of circumstances, you can change your life by as much as you like — by learning new skills, and by applying yourself as fully as you can — with intelligence and intuition, and with *intent*.

Each new skill acquired will give you more confidence; what is more, if you apply one skill well, then you will find other skills easier to master. Then you can go about the business of restructuring your life in a way that will give you more and more energy; and this will also become the platform you will need in order to explore your potential — not only with regard to venturing out onto other levels of existence — in your consciousness — and learning from that experience, but also with respect to maximising things for yourself within the mundane or ordinary world.

Furthermore, in time you will come to realise how connected these two are — the one reinforces the results gained by doing the other.

This is a part of the *vital experiment* — beforehand you may not actually know what you are capable of, or what you can manifest for yourself, or how to go about doing things initially — particularly if you feel inept, or else without enough experience and power with regard to changing *what is* into *what will be*, or into *what needs to be*.

Be prepared for the efforts that you will have to make: it will take you some time before you manage to manifest what you need, or what you want. Do not expect instant change as of right — in fact what is ahead of you may seem to be like a tall, Himalayan mountain, whose peak disappears amongst the clouds! And here you are, more or less naked, and without any climbing equipment; and without any climbing experience.

And you have never climbed that sort of mountain before; it seems awesome — and its peak appears to be unreachable.

Everyone who *has not* feels like that to begin with. Then as you master one *doing* relatively well, it permits you to master something else. Each thing done well gives you added discipline, and added skills — and added strength.

In time this begins to accumulate — and then things become easier and easier, even though the challenges may also become progressively more difficult.

15 — PLANNING

One can either do things in a completely spontaneous manner, or else one can make plans; or one can do a bit of both.

Doing things on a spontaneous basis can be great fun, yet it may not always *add up* to anything very coherent in the end.

Whereas over-planning may lead to a rigid format of expression which will cause you to miss out on a variety of possibilities which are best accessed in a spontaneous fashion.

Therefore you need to be able to *think* and *feel* — mentate and intuit — and this at all times, and in synchronicity; or else alternately, as may be necessary.

If you have a project in mind, you can begin to structure the way that you are going to approach it, and then deal with it. First of all you need to define to yourself what the project consists of in general; then you need to isolate the main constituent parts of that project; then develop the detail of each of those parts, starting with the first.

This will give you a working, detailed outline of your project.

An example: in terms of this book, the project is defined as *THE POWER OF CREATIVE VISUALISATION*, the constituent parts are the various chapters and sections; and the detail is the text.

That is the way it was conceived, to begin with — first came the idea, with regard to creative visualisation, and the title suggested itself; next I wrote a brief outline which consisted of five chapter headings; then I filled in that outline with a number of sections which would permit me to highlight different facets pertaining to creative visualisation; and finally I got down to the business of writing the text and the information (the hardest part!).

If I had not bothered with creating the outline, then I would not have had the *perspective* which I needed in order to write this book.

Above all else an outline will clarify your mind with regard to what you propose to do. Once that clarity exists it will make your *doing* a lot easier — you will have laid down your tracks, and all that you will need to do from there onwards is to follow them through and apply yourself as you go along, and this as meticulously as possible — making amendments wherever necessary, yet without destroying the structure of the whole outline. If radical amendments appear to be desirable in the light of more experience, it is usually best to draft a new outline, while preserving everything which was good or useful about the first or initial effort.

All this, of course, just makes sense. Nevertheless it is amazing how many people will ignore the need for making a detailed outline of their projects; as a result their projects become confused — because they are confused — and this tends to lead to more and more chaos; and usually to the breakdown of the entire project itself, in each instance.

16 — SETTING UP

Once a satisfactory outline has been produced there may still be areas which require further clarification — for example (and we will consider here the average needs of a mundane business), what sort of tools are needed in order to implement the project? Which tools are the best ones within a given price range for the type of project that you wish to initiate? Where can you get these tools from?

If the project requires finances, where can you get these from? Is it best to buy items outright, or is it best to lease or hire, or purchase these on credit? How much money will be needed for insurance, specialised services, advertising, etc? (Most banks have booklets which cover all these mundane points).

Answers to these questions often necessitates careful consideration — you don't want to reach a situation where you overstretch yourself early on; your project, if it is financially based, will need a financial outline, and this will have to be as balanced and as accurate as possible, and within your means (if you manage to increase those means through creative visualisation, so much the better).

If your project is more subjectively oriented, an outline is still very valuable.

17 — WORKING

Once you have an outline which covers the initial thrust of your intended project you can get down to some work. Here again there is a need for an outline — one which in effect will cover the *way* that you are actually going to work.

Where are you going to work? How many hours are you going to work per day or per week? How much time is each element of the project likely to take before it is fulfilled? What sort of schedule will you need to implement?

Will you be able to avoid distractions? Will your work put pressure on you personally, and perhaps on others as well (too much work to be done in too short a time; strain on personal relationships; too many *different* things to think about and do, etc)?

Invariably difficulties will arise, therefore you will want to be able to cater for these, and be prepared for them — and this as adequately as possible.

Let us look at some of these points — they are potentially less easy to deal with than you may think.

Where are you going to work? Is it going to be a place which is conducive to your work? Will it provide you with enough practical *space* to move around in and/or store things, as may be necessary? This in itself can become a major preoccupation, i.e., just getting the setting right.

Are you the sort of person who likes to work from 9 to 5 each day? Or do you prefer the idea of working when you like — i.e., of stopping and starting as you may feel the need or the inclination, in which case have you got enough discipline to make that a viable proposition?

Working from 9 to 5 is a practical thing to do — or is it? It may *not* be in your case; and it can be very boring working like that anyway. What if you suddenly have a stroke of genius at one minute to five? Are you going to stop working just because five o'clock is imminent?!

Likewise you can take it for granted that it will practically always take you somewhat longer to fulfil a project than you may have thought was necessary at the outset. Almost everyone misjudges this point, including most experienced professionals. This misjudgement may put you under some pressure, and perhaps even under *intense* pressure — particularly if you have a deadline to meet. Then the deadline comes and goes, and you set up a new deadline, and you may well find yourself unable to meet that one as well; and then you start to become frustrated and tired, perhaps irritated, and you can no longer work properly — which delays things even further.

And you may miss various opportunities in the process. Maybe you will lose sales, because somebody else comes up with a product of a similar kind before you do, markets it sooner, and reaps all the benefits. A contract may become void, because you were unable to deliver the goods on time. Or perhaps the delays merely create absolute chaos, in some manner.

Do not underestimate the possibilities of becoming distracted either. Perhaps the phone rings incessantly, and those who are on the other end of the line want to speak to *you*, and to no one else; or people visit you unexpectedly; or your partner in life, if you have one, comes and unloads all hir problems on you? Or whatever.

And of course you may be quite adept at distracting yourself, without any extra outside assistance being involved in any manner whatsoever!

Sometimes the delays which may occur will not be your particular fault in any way at all, or have anything to do with the way you tend to work. A tool that you are using — say, a computer — may malfunction or corrupt your hard disk, and days or weeks, or even months of hard work will be lost... unless you did what anyone should do, and therefore you took the sensible precaution of backing up your data on floppies as well; more delay, because your computer now requires servicing; have you got a servicing contract? If not, how much is it going to cost you to get it fixed? Can you afford it? Yet it must be repaired, otherwise your project is going to collapse. Or perhaps the delivery of essential supplies may get delayed; supplies you ordered and then received may not work properly, or else may be the wrong kind of supplies — all these types of difficulties, and many possible others, will upset your schedule.

It is not always possible to anticipate all the kinds of trouble you may experience one way or another. However, difficulties are not always the bane that they may appear to be — a mishap can lead to a realisation, to a re-evaluation of your efforts, to a new way of doing something, to a greater flexibility.

For instance, you may learn not to invoke difficulties!

18 — LEARNING FROM EXPERIENCE

Whatever you have chosen to do, or whatever it is that you choose to do in the future, you will learn something from it. If something goes wrong, you will have to discover and understand why it went wrong.

As you learn and/or apply a skill, you will find ways of doing things better. This in turn will give you new ideas, which you can set out to experiment with; and each experiment, regardless of whether it is successful or not, will teach you a new angle.

This applies as much to one's Spiritual and psychic explorations as it does to running a business, or being involved in any mundane venture; and the main point here is that practising creative visualisation is one of the *tool* which will help you to make the process far more accessible, and far more rewarding as well.

Each vision that you have in meditation may seem compelling in itself; in meditation you will probably come across all sorts of ideas, and each one of these could lead to a project, or maybe several. Some of these will seem viable, while others may not appear quite so feasible; you will have to select those which you want to work with, and then make notes with regard to the rest — they may become useful later on, however.

Learning from experience also means that you will sometimes

find yourself thrown in at the deep end — you may have to learn a skill from scratch, and perhaps learn it within a fairly short space of time as well. For example, in order to carry out a particular task you may have to learn to use a complex computer program within a week or two, and this may infringe upon your work schedule. How can you best learn this program while continuing with you work?

This is when you will have to divide your time usefully — and manage to do both.

But let us say that you have difficulties in understanding how the program works, and that the manual provided is ill-documented; or that the program does not behave as described in that manual — what then? Is the program faulty (does it have *bugs*)? Are you sure you are doing what is suggested? Have you been pressing the wrong keys?

These tribulations, and many others like them, of whatever kind, will eat up your time. Finally you come to the conclusion that the program is faulty. In desperation you may resort to sending it back to the company which produced it, or to the distributor, asking them to replace it with a working copy as soon as possible — that is, immediately! They may not answer you for days or weeks.

Meanwhile your schedule has been disrupted.

From this you may learn to be that much more flexible, and not to depend on any one tool wherever possible. You will feel justified in acquiring back-up tools, or alternative ones.

However, initially you may not have the resources to do this. Or you may go and buy tools which subsequently you will never use.

All this will form the background of your experience. After a while you will be much wiser about what to do, when, and why, given any number of different situations or difficulties — and this applies to a subjective application as it does to a mundane project.

You will also learn how to, say, advertise. If one advertisement does not work well for you, you will wonder why. Was it a good advertisement? Was it well presented? Did it describe your wares in the best possible fashion, without resorting to massive expenses? Did you advertise in the right publication(s)? Were you trying to sell goods which others are selling cheaper? How similar are your goods to those produced by other companies? And so on.

Whenever feasible, your project needs to be as unique as possible; your goods need to reflect something special; the way that you present them need to be pertinent; the publications you use for advertising purposes must reach the type of people who are likely to feel inspired by what you have to sell.

Later we will discuss something of the ethics of New Age business (see Appendix).

You will also learn a lot from your successes — yet what is successful at any one given time may not remain that way. You will have to innovate continuously.

You will need to learn from the feedback you may get from those who buy your goods, and listen to what they want, or what they say they need.

19 — STRUCTURAL THOUGHTS

Building up a project is much like the growth of a tree. One decision leads to another. From out of the *roots* of your idea a *tree* will be born, which will eventually branch out in various directions

You will need to organise your thoughts in the same way — going from one thing to another, logically, intuitively, and dynamically.

Structuring thoughts can be done simply — find a piece of paper. Describe to yourself what your *roots* are; this will be the *bubble* at the top of your page. The *trunk* of your tree will represent the main thrust of the project, and it must be capable of supporting all the subsequent elements of your scheme; this is the second *bubble*. Then you will have the main branches of the project (a number of different *bubbles,* representing the main categories within that scheme). Finally you may create a great many smaller *bubbles*, which will represent a variety of different goods, or whatever.

In time, as the project unfolds, you will obtain *flowers*, and then *fruit* — these will represent your successes, i.e., the return on your investment of time and energy, including the use of creative visualisation and meditation.

Although much of this is written with business applications in mind, it does not prevent you from adapting the principles involved to suit more subjective needs.

20 — APPLICATION

Once your structural thoughts are sound you can give yourself over to the work of applying them. You can avoid many difficulties by being aware of all the potential set-backs which could interfere with the smooth unfoldment of your project; and by thinking about your project in as much depth as possible.

This is where creative visualisation can be very useful — on the one hand you can evolve a project in your mind, and then look at all the creative inputs that you will need to inject into your scheme; and on the other hand you can anticipate some of the potential difficulties which you may have to cope with... and perhaps this way you may be able to avoid them altogether.

Whatever you do, do not rush your project into existence this often leads to immediate problems. Once you have designed the mainframe of your scheme, give yourself time to consider it more fully. What may have seemed *good* and viable one day, a few days later may not appear to be quite so viable; your enthusiasm may blind you to the reality of what is at stake. Conversely, you do not want to lose your enthusiasm for a project by invoking untold difficulties either — some of these difficulties can be fairly easily dealt with as soon as you begin to apply yourself anyway; others may require more thought, more intuition, and more experience; and all these need to be aligned with your *intent*.

Ambivalence can be a great danger — i.e., changing your mind too frequently. You may decide on a range of goods, start working on them, then a few days or weeks later you end up changing them — redefining them, re-working them, re-pricing them, etc. This can be a great waste of time and energy, and sometimes can be very costly; if you have already advertised them this will confuse prospective customers as well, which may become reflected as a lack of confidence on their part, and therefore lead to a lack of sales.

Whatever you choose to do, try and be consistent. Only make those changes which are absolutely vital.

There will be times when you will have to make changes either because the costs of the raw materials have gone up; or because you had underestimated your production expenses; or because you want to upgrade your products; and so on.

Avoid advertising your goods in advance — even if you believe that you will be able to fulfil production before people actually start ordering. Delays may well alienate your customers. If unavoidable delays do occur, think of compensating your customers in some way — by offering them something for free as a token of your goodwill, for example.

There are legal requirements which you will need to acquaint yourself with. For instance, if your business is mail order based you must despatch an order within 28 days of receiving it. If for some reason you cannot do so, you must advise your customers as to when you are likely to be able to fulfil the orders, and offer them a full refund; if they write to you or phone you and say that they want a refund, you must send them their money back immediately, regardless of any inconvenience to yourself. Later you can advise them with regard to the availability of the product(s), and give them the option of reordering if they so wish.

If you are clear and fair about what you say to your customers, and offer them the option of a full refund (which is a legal prerequisite anyway), it is usually the case that they will not ask for that refund, and will be prepared to wait for the availability of the products.

Nevertheless, technically, it is illegal to advertise a product which is not yet available, although many companies infringe on this requirement — it may not be intentional on their part, but they stand to be taken to court if they do not advise their customers of any delays, and offer a prompt, unconditional and courteous refund as an option.

It is not the purpose of this book to itemise all the legal requirements with respect to business transactions. If in doubt, then consult a solicitor.

(With regard to mail order business, RUNNING YOUR OWN MAIL ORDER BUSINESS by Malcolm Breckman, published by Kogan Page, is a useful book to read — which also contains a lot of other information appertaining to other types of business.)

The application of an idea or project is always much harder than the devising of it in the first place. Allow for this. Against this, the rewards in personal terms for a successful venture can be enormous — not just financially, but as a matter of learning, then mastering new skills, all of which will lead to a new sense of self-confidence. Also, doing what you want to do can be very enjoyable.

21 — ECONOMY v. RISK

At the outset of a financially based project it is tempting to avail oneself of all sorts of facilities — yet this can not only be costly, it can lead to more difficulties than it is worth. There needs to be an emphasis on economy whenever possible. Some people like to gamble, but most gamblers fall foul of these difficulties.

Nevertheless there will be times when risks seem viable. If you should feel drawn to take a risk then calculate that risk as carefully as you can, and make contingency plans should things go wrong.

Conversely, being too economical can sometimes strangle the flow of the project. Once again there is a need for balance.

This is another reason why planning is so important — it will help you to know when to economise, and when to take risks.

22 — LOOKING AT ALL THE ASPECTS OF AN ENTERPRISE

Many businesses fail because those in control of these businesses fail to look at all the aspects of their ventures. This may happen because they take certain things for granted, when these cannot be taken for granted.

Each and all aspects of a project should be kept under periodical review. If something is not working as it should, solutions must be found.

Big businesses sometimes have the greatest difficulties, particularly large manufacturing concerns. As they spread themselves by creating more and more departments (sometimes located in different places), communication between one department and another almost invariably breaks down — the left hand no longer knows what the right is doing, and vice-versa; each person and each department becomes too involved in its own particular preoccupations. Management may endorse a view which is not put clearly to the workers, or even to their immediate subordinates, and the workers may be aware of problems to which the management is completely insensitive. Relations between the two become increasingly fraught, to the extent that they may no longer exist.

What is true of large companies can also be true of your own mind.

When things go wrong, and it starts to tell on sales, big companies have to bring in one or more consultants to sort out the mess — these consultants will then make it their business to spend some time in each department looking for the flaws in the whole operation, and eventually they will report their findings to the management and make recommendations with regard to alleviating the problems.

In your case you may have to be management, worker and consultant all rolled into one. You will have to make sure that you keep all the communication lines open within your own mind and consciousness; do not go so far as to neglect any aspect of your venture — if you do, it will become your Achilles heel; do not get so involved in one part of the project that all the others suffer as a consequence.

If you have problems which you cannot sort out yourself, then get the advice of a professional consultant. There are many consultancy services, usually regional ones, which cater for small businesses; many of these charge very little, and in some cases nothing at all — particularly if you are on the Enterprise Allowance Scheme (U.K.).

23 — *THE LOGICAL CHOICE v. THE INTUITIVE CHOICE*

A logical choice is one that makes sense to the mind; whereas an intuitive choice is one which is perceived with the i*nner eye*.

The one need not exclude the other, yet there will be times when there may appear to be a contradiction between what the mind thinks, and what your intuition reveals.

You may *feel* that you should do a particular thing, but your mind says *No*; or your intuition may say *No*, but your mind says *Yes*. If you reach such an impasse you will have to look deeper into what is causing this lack of accord.

The mind tends to say that something is right or wrong as based on its previous experience. It may be right, in relative terms, or else it may be suffering from a conditioning block. If that block exists it will need to be examined very carefully, and the mind will have to be *shown* that it is wrong.

One's intuition may also be right or wrong. Intuitive perception depends largely on internal clarity and sensitivity. If the sensitivity is at fault, then the intuition will be obscured in direct proportion to this. Also, it is easy to mistake an emotional appeal for an intuition.

True intuition *feels right*; and if your mind is clear, it will be interpreted as *right* by the mind as well. Intuition is not only a *feeling*, however — it is a type of Spiritual insight. When the mind is in *alignment* with that inner sight, it sees clearly itself, and therefore endorses the intuition.

CHAPTER 4 — CREATIVE INSPIRATION

24 — THE SPIRIT

One can view life in many different ways, and one's own personal view may be highly complex, or else it may be very simple. One can *feel* Spiritually inclined, or one can be totally materialistic; or anything more or less in between.

Different things may inspire each one of us — an aesthetic idea in itself is inspiring; walking through a wood can be inspiring; viewing someone's artwork can trigger off all sorts of impressions; a piece of information can jolt some fundamental *recognition* process within oneself.

Nevertheless it is the *spirit of things* which inspires us; one needs to *feel* the Spirit within oneself; one needs to *feel* the Spirit around oneself...

As a creative spirit one needs inspiration — and the word, *inspiration* is directly related to the word *Spirit*; *inspiration* comes from the Latin word, *spirare*, to breathe.

One needs to *breathe Life* into oneself — and only then is it possible to create something which is worthwhile, by *breathing life* into it.

In Theosophy — a view system inherited from the ancient Tibetans — the Spirit is the *Atma*; the first Aspect of the Higher Self, representing Will, Purpose, Power, Force and *Intent*.

From one point of view one can think of Atma as *Spiritual electricity*; whereas the Buddhic Plane, or *Buddhi* — the Plane *below* Atma — can be thought of as *Spiritual magnetic energy*, representing Interconnectedness, Love, Intuition, Quality and Harmony. The Higher Mind (or Higher *Manas*), in turn, can be thought of as *Spiritual friction-fire* — which friction represents the power of the Mind to create complementary-opposites; and therefore the Mind is the Creator/Creatrix Aspect of Spirit.

All three of these Spiritual Aspects can inspire, singly, or in tandem.

And all three are Aspects of the Monad — or the *One Self*; the *God-dess within*; the *Seed of Existence*; the *All-pervading Essence*... which are esoteric names for the Spirit.

None of this will mean much to anyone who has not actually experienced these three Aspects, directly and in full consciousness. They represent *Planes of Consciousness* — formless worlds which interpenetrate the world that we know, and on which we are presently incarnate.

Since the average intellect alone cannot grasp what Atma and Buddhi are about without becoming *aligned* in consciousness with these, to try and define these matters in mental terms might be considered a waste of time.

However a bit of *parallel processing* may come to the rescue.

Friction fire — representing the Mind — is easy enough to understand. The Mind operates by comparing various sets of complementary-opposites, which it creates by virtue of its expression. Thus *male* and *female*, *black* and *white*, *human* and *deva*, *high* and *low*, *right* and *left*, *logic* and *illogic*, etc, are all complementary-opposites which the Mind can work with — with relish. The Mind would not be the Mind without them!

When a given set is in opposition mode, it creates friction; and therefore heat. It is simple enough to understand this from one angle.

The Mind thereby provides us with the facility of being able to compare two apparently opposite aspects of a single principle, and thereby make judgments with regard to where our interests lie.

The Buddhi does not do this at all — quite on the contrary; the Buddhi cannot divide things into opposites or complementaries. It is a principle of *Union*; and here at least rests a hint with regard to its magnetic properties.

To experience Buddhi is to experience the *Unity of all things*; in Buddhic consciousness there are no paradoxes. All complementary-opposites are seen and experienced as *One*. This is also why Buddhic consciousness is so blissful — there are no mental schisms to be endured, and no paradoxes to be resolved. In this state one only feels pure, unequivocal Love and Affinity for all Life.

To experience Atma, however, is to feel the *pure intensity* of the Spirit — i.e., pure Force, or Power. When ignited by Atmic energies one feels full of Will and Purpose, and *Intent*; one senses an inherent *alignment* within oneself between one's individuality and the Planetary and Cosmic Self.

Once again, (the Higher) Mind, Buddhi and Atma are the three Key Aspects of the Monad.

Becoming conscious of these three Aspects of the Spirit/ Higher Self is inspiration enough to motivate any number of excellent projects — with the needs of the planet in mind.

Once one has been *touched* by the Spirit one cannot remain self-centred to the point of selfishness any longer. One realises that o*ne is a part of the Spirit*, and that the planet is a part of the Spirit also; therefore one begins to work consciously on behalf of the Spirit, and by extension on behalf of the planet as well.

... And then one can draw on the Spirit for inspiration, and this at any time...

25 — THE SOLAR DEVA

One's Solar Deva is the direct counterpart of one's human self, or human spirit. S/he is one's *other half,* as it were. S/he is one's Soul, from one angle — in fact one's Soul (Sol; Solar; Sun) is the *human spirit* side of one's Solar Deva; and one's lower self, or personality self, is a small fragment of both — which has been *precipitated into lower existence for the sake of acquiring individuality,* because one's Soul/Solar Deva, in hirself and on hir own level, is incapable of individuality — s/he is a being whose consciousness is purely collective or unitive in nature.

It is only by fusing oneself, in consciousness, with one's Solar Deva that s/he acquires individuality, yet s/he also remains a *unitive and collective being.*

In turn again, one's Solar Deva/Soul is a fragment of a Higher

Soul — the Cosmic Deva, or Cosmic Soul (or MahaDeva).

Much inspiration can pass down that line!

To become fully conscious of one's Solar Deva is an utterly beautiful, and ecstatic, and powerful experience. Any projects considered in the Light of that conscious contact will take on *Wings of Light and a Heart of Fiery Love,* as one esoteric aphorism puts it.

Some people call the Solar Deva the Solar Angel.

Once acknowledged, one's Solar Deva becomes an active *ally* in one's life and one's work. Bit by bit the closeness between one's personality self and one's Solar Deva becomes more and more pronounced — until one eventually merges, in full consciousness, with one's Solar Deva; and thus accesses a freedom which few of us can even imagine, alone understand.

Much of this is covered in THE PSYCHIC EXPLORER, in STARCRAFT, and in the other two books which have been bundled with this one.

26 — EXTRA-DIMENSIONALS

Whatever is not in physical incarnation can be thought of as extra-dimensional. Nevertheless, here we are referring principally to those Spiritual entities who live and have their being on those Planes which are higher than the lower Mental Plane. These too can be the source of an enormous amount of inspiration — providing an *alignment* with these is made at a conscious level.

All these beings are *of the Spirit;* therefore they work on behalf of the planet, or even the Solar System, or on behalf of other planetary and stellar Beings. Their purpose is always united with that of these heavenly Beings, whose Purpose in turn is always united with that of the Cosmic Being, or Cosmic God-dess.

There is only One Higher Self. If a being is genuinely in *alignment* with That, then that is a being which can be trusted. The only Way to *know* if a being is in *alignment* with the Higher Self is to be in *alignment* with It oneself; then like recognises like.

27 — *THE REAL* FACE *BEHIND THE MASK*

Within each one of us is the One Being — call That the Goddess, the Cosmic Self, Reality, Life, or whatever... Behind the *mask of appearances*, otherwise known as the *veil of illusion* (Maya), our Higher Self can be found, and can be accessed; one can then become consciously identified with Hir/It/Life.

Needless to say, if inspiration is needed this is a fairly good place to go and find it!

28 — *ALIGNMENT AND IDENTITY*

So far in this chapter only little *memos* have been outlined (memos at least for those who have read the other books in this range).

The greatest usefulness of meditation is that it can permit us to access other levels of Self, and this through *alignment*. Each level of Self has its own identity — one of consciousness. As we become *aligned* with another level of Self and change our consciousness accordingly, we take on (at least something of) its identity.

This identity should not be confused with personality identity; it is something far more Spiritual than that. However, when this occurs, one's personality identity becomes temporarily fused with the higher identity. One partakes of one's God-dess Aspect at some level or other (higher Mind, Buddhi, or Atma); if one goes a little further — an event which occurs at the first Life-Initiation — one then becomes identified with one's Monad. This is a stupendous experience, and it leaves one without any doubt whatsoever with regard to what is truly *Real*.

In the context of inspiration, being conscious of the Monad — by being *aligned* with It — gives one all the possible inspiration one may require for a whole lifetime's work; the books in this series were all inspired by this type of *alignment*.

Meeting one's Monad for the first time at a conscious level is a devastating experience, not just a stupendous one. The power involved in this *realisation* is colossal. As a result, because of the sheer strain of it, the *meeting* does not take place for very long — a few hours at most.

It's a struggle to get that far; one's spine is afire with Kundalini, and initially one is fully preoccupied with adapting one's lower energies to the impact of the higher energies involved; Spiritual Agencies act as guides, and visual to telepathic disclosures are made (often in momentary flashes). One's mind becomes largely abstracted. The whole foundation of one's personality is rattled and altered immeasurably. One's consciousness spirals upwards, and upwards (in figurative terms), and the only way forward is to trust and surrender to this Force. To flow with It. One begins to emerge at the top of the spiral; energies begin to find their balance; the Power becomes more refined... Then Life imparts a vision of its Manifesting Principle — and it does so in a very simple, very direct, very friendly and truly exquisite manner... Finally, once *there* — on what may be called a *Monadic Plateau* — the struggle comes to something of an end; one cannot relax yet, and one's consciousness is still unfolding in layer after layer — one *sees* a Cosmic vista. Aeonic time. A superlative Now. And one realises that one is God-dess. That one is *It*; and that one has always been *It* — within oneself, and however unrecognised this fact may have been previously.

Oneness.

Millions of years ago, prior to individualisation, one was *That* — in that State of Consciousness; undifferentiated, and at-One with the Spirit.

Everything one sees is awash with Power and beauty... all the external energy-forms are gliding, merging, and fusing into one another — overlaid with higher energies; dancing, colourful, *revealed* — their Devic Essence is then no longer veiled to one's sight.

One's individuality is now fused with the Monadic Self (temporarily).

Readjusting to everyday life after that is perhaps even more difficult — not because it produces a greater struggle, but once the *Heights* have been visited it is hard indeed to have to relinquish that sublime *State of Consciousness* — until the next time; until the next Life-Initiation, when other things will be *seen*, experienced, and realised.

After this particular ordeal one knows that a day will come when one will lift one's consciousness out of the physical world and onto that Higher Level — permanently; and then move on beyond that in time into even greater Heights...

You might think that after such an experience that all one's personal life would come effortlessly into perspective; that all one's troubles would be over. Not so. One's personality self still needs to carry on from where it left off... although at least it has now been exposed to something so transcendental and so undeniable that it is not likely to forget it.

In the process the levels and qualities of all one's energies have been altered as well.

CHAPTER 5 — THE ESOTERIC ASPECTS OF CREATIVITY

29 — *LIFE AS AN EVOLUTIONARY UNFOLDMENT*

Who can say how Life began in the first place? Regardless of such theories as the *Big Bang* and the *Steady State*, from a mundane viewpoint we really know very little about the original impulse behind the Creation of the Cosmos.

From an esoteric vantage one can discern certain abstractions which do make things somewhat more understandable, in an intuitive way — they are not necessarily easy to acknowledge at an intellectual level because the mind automatically seeks chains of causes and effects — i.e., it automatically becomes involved in dualism.

Consider an abstraction which includes no time and no space — a *place* which is not really a place as we know it — a *State* (and it is not even that) which has no form, no dimensional characteristics whatsoever, and it is not energy either (energy can only exist in time and space). Therefore there is no movement at all; no manifestation; not even an essence.

To say that it has the *Potential for Manifestation* sounds paradoxical. One cannot even call it the *Void*. Nevertheless, from out of this *State* comes everything that is.

Esotericists in different ages and cultures have grappled with this abstraction. Definitions like the *Voidless Void*, the *Source*, *Nothingness*, and the *Point of Potential* have all been used in an attempt to describe *It*.

However, a word like *Potential* is misleading. A dictionary defines potential as *latent; existing in possibility but not in actuality; inherent capability of doing anything*. Yet how can *It* be latent if it is not actually there at all? How can *It* represent a possibility, let alone a future actuality? How can *It* have any inherent capability of doing anything?

One can then think of *It* as a *Zero State* — yet It is not a *state*; a state implies a condition. Here there is no condition.

If we admit for the time being that we are not going to find the perfect word or definition for *It*, how does a *Zero State* become something else than *Nothingness/Void?* How does this *Potential* become manifest in any way?

One cannot invoke an *Act of Will*— not at a primordial level — because there is nothing here to express that *Will*. Nor is It an *Act of Love,* because there is nothing which loves, or to be loved. Nor is It an *Act of Mind,* because there is no Mind.

It is the greatest Mystery of all.

It is far easier to consider Manifestation and to say that Life *has always been*, regardless of the enormity of that notion — that is, there was no beginning, and there will be no end. A *Steady State*.

Maybe a *Cyclical State*.

Tibetan esotericism tells us that the Universe goes through a period of Manifestation, then dissolves and enters *Pralaya* (Period of Quiescence) — during *Pralaya* the Universe is abstracted. It is still active on a much higher Level, but it is no longer manifest. It is at rest. For all intents and purposes, it is discarnate.

Ancient Tibetan Initiates said of It that at these times *It is dreaming*.

This Tibetan view then compares this with the breathing out and the breathing in of the Cosmic Life. During the out-breath the possibilities are sown; during the in-breath the actualities are harvested, and are resolved and synthesised into (a type of) Supreme Consciousness.

In this light all Manifestation is about evolving Consciousness; the process of Emergence into Manifestation, Immersion in Manifestation, then Transcendence and the Abstraction or Withdrawal of Life from Manifestation, is a three-fold *Act of Need* — the need for REALISED Consciousness, plus the ability to Will and to Act/Create.

Still paraphrasing from these Tibetan insights, it is said that the Sun is presently in its second Incarnation, and is evolving

Cosmic Consciousness; whereas in its previous Incarnation it evolved Cosmic Mind, or Cosmic Creativity; and that in its third Incarnation, yet to come, it will evolve Cosmic Will.

30 — SPIRALS WITHIN SPIRALS

One can view Emergence as a gradual *Descent of the Life Spiral* into denser and denser zones of Manifestation, which it creates as it goes along (see STARCRAFT), followed by a period of Immersion whereby the Spirit can individualise Itself into an infinite number of individual beings (including yourself reading this), followed by Transcendence — each individual consciously reintegrating hirself with the Cosmic Oneness, and without losing hir ability to be an individual; this represents the *Ascent of the Life Spiral*.

The whole process is one of spirals within spiral — both during the Descent and the Ascent; the same could be said of natural evolution.

31 — GRADUALLY INCARNATING...

Many people who acknowledge reincarnation think of it as something which happens at physical birth; then the individual unfolds into physical life.

Another way of perceiving reincarnation, particularly in the case of advanced individuals, is to see it as a gradual process: at physical birth the individualised spirit begins to incarnate, then gradually incarnates more and more of himself, and finally s/he will bring the full force of hir realised potential into manifestation; as a result s/he will begin to live more fully, and s/he will then unfold that potential further.

If hir realised potential is great enough s/he will experience various stages of Life-Initiation, culminating eventually in personal transcendence.

Full realised human potential requires a mastery of Creativity, Intuition/Consciousness and Will.

32 — PART OF THE COSMIC NETWORK

When the fully realised human (now fused with hir Solar Deva, therefore fully androgynous) transcends the limitations of lower manifestation, s/he eventually takes up *residence* in the Monadic State and becomes a fully fledged agent on behalf of the Cosmic Network (see THE PSYCHIC EXPLORER; STARCRAFT; and MEDITATIONS and JOURNEYING — A PATH OF SELF-DISCOVERY, which follow). S/he has then actualised hir ability to be a Cosmic Creator/Creatrix.

Although this book has concentrated somewhat on the more mundane applications of creative visualisation, its true import is in instigating one's preparation to become a Cosmic Creatorix (an new *androgynous* word for the New Age dictionary, if you will) — at-One with The Creative Essence or Being. In potential we are already That; now we have to realise It — and actualise It within ourselves.

MEDITATIONS, which follows, was written with this in mind.

Being a conscious, functioning part or agent on behalf of the Cosmic Network entails work which is too far removed from the human state to be fully considered here. It is the actualisation of everything we have learnt to the nth degree.

33 — THE PEACE WITHIN

Pure meditation facilitates the movement of consciousness into a state where there is no movement — thereby approximating the *Zero State*. Within that State there is nothing but ultimate Peace.

This is a State that all Cosmic Creatorixes need to be able to access at *will* before they act outwardly and manifest their schemes.

It is the *Central Reference Point*.

(See Section 20, THE COSMIC GOD-DESS, in THE PSYCHIC EXPLORER.)

34 — OTHER LEVELS OF CONSCIOUSNESS

Within the Seven Planes that we have access to (etheric-physical; Astral; Mental; Buddhic; Atm(a)ic; Monadic and Ad(a)ic) there are *Seven Key Types* of Consciousness, each one of which has seven sub-zones, or sub-layers of Consciousness.

When the *Seven Key Types* of Consciousness are realised, they are fused and synthesised into an *Eighth Key State of Consciousness,* and one escapes from the Seven Planes into Higher Cosmic Planes — each one of These representing a certain Cosmic State of Consciousness.

These we will have to actualise for ourselves as well — in the due course of our Cosmic Evolution.

35 — JOY!

To actualise our Spiritual potential is the most joyous act possible. May THE POWER OF CREATIVE VISUALISATION be yours!

APPENDIX

NEW AGE ETHICS IN BUSINESS AND POLITICS

What does all this information point to if we consider the New Age, and particularly if we consider the ethics of New Age business and politics?

At present businesses rely on competition rather than on co-operation, although a measure of co-operation does exist in some instances, from a certain angle of view at least. If we accept that we can and need to be unitive in our approach — that humanity as a whole is a holistic unit, and that together we can derive all our needs in every department of human and global life, and solve our more demanding problems — including attending to matters of ecology — then we can begin to phase out competition by initiating collective acts, i.e., by working together, thereby maximising our potential for creativity as living beings.

Again, at present businesses rely on profits in order to grow and expand — and rely on a monetary system, which though purely illusionary from one point of view, has a stated value which we give to it. By giving it this value we collectively and effectively create money with money, via a process of commercialism — making, selling and buying goods, services and shares in companies, etc.

The Gross National Product (GNP) of any one country is its total annual production; this in turn consists of *visible* and so-called *invisible* earnings (*invisible* ones are principally related to bank interests and insurance). As the GNP grows, the money supply and reserves become greater, and it then permits that country to spend more on whatever it wants (including armaments, for instance — for itself; and it will also try and sell weapons and weapon-related devices to other countries in order to: (1) derive profits and recoup on its research and development expenses, and on its production expenses; (2) for political reasons).

A substantial percentage of this GNP is wasted on things that ideally nobody in hir right mind really wants and/or needs; and as a result resources which could be used to enhance our lives are simply not made available.

An example: in 1987 the US administration requested the US Congress to ratify a defense spending of over $1,000,000,000,000 (one million million, or one trillion dollars — NB: Americans call 1,000 million a trillion). Imagine what could be done with this money in creative terms; in fact it is staggering to think of such utter waste. The US government is attempting to instigate fears within the minds of the US people (not to mention anyone else) in order to levy this huge sum of money with view to subsidising its infamous *Star Wars* or SDI (Strategic Defense Initiative) projects, amongst other things.

Regardless of whether the technology involved will lead to benefits in the end — for instance, the design and manufacture of starships, and various spin off technologies — the declared motivation for the *Star Wars*/SDI projects is both negative and totally insane.

In 1988, Gorbachev, the Soviet leader, invited all nations to join together in a global Space Project, which would eventually lead to full co-operation in Space exploration, and to all the benefits thereof — to be shared and mutually accessed; which is a very positive and very sane, and intelligent proposition.

No one in hir right mind (remember the right brain?!) wants nuclear war, and no one wants war in space either no one can benefit from that in itself. Instead of consolidating on the goodwill which can pass between East and West — especially now that the Soviet Union is moving towards its own form of democracy under a more enlightened leadership — the US administration appears to be still bent on the idea of supremacy, regardless of cost, forcing the Soviets to consider adequate moves to prevent that US supremacy... although the US, and the West generally, is now gradually realising that Gorbachev actually means what he says, that he wants peace for the world, and that he realises only too well that no one nation can rule the planet — it is a profitless folly.

Meanwhile one can sense that the people of Europe are getting increasingly tired of the US administration's belligerence, and they perceive that the Soviets are making most of the positive moves towards genuine peace (they do not excuse Soviet excesses, yet they can easily draw their own conclusions with regard to who is doing the most towards healing the rift between East and West; it is patently evident).

Western Europe so far has been in the middle, though to date remains militarily, economically and politically affiliated with the United States. Nevertheless, Western Europe is now gradually becoming more and more independent of US political views, and is therefore seeking its own integrity as a political, economical and military power. Fewer and fewer Europeans still harbour the illusion that the USA would effectively protect them against a Soviet military invasion — which in itself is extremely unlikely, since the Soviet Union could not possibly gain anything whatsoever from invading Western Europe. Aside from any other reasons, and there are plenty of them, its economy is far too fragile to entertain this possibility or idea.

The original reason for the Soviets' build-up of military strength was to prevent the Soviet Union ever being invaded again, and suffering the dire consequences at the hands of invaders; something which non-native Americans have not experienced for themselves (the Amerindians are still suffering the consequences, however).

All these matters concern us all, regardless of which country we live in.

The schism between East and West is healing, and yet what has prevailed for decades now exemplifies the stupidity of competition, as distinct from co-operation and mutuality.

In the business world competition does not involve the possibility of global genocide, although it does suffer from a tendency towards corporate monopolies and powerful cartels. Until we genuinely perceive that this is not what we want or need either — from a collective point of view — we will go on paying the price of this other stupidity... mostly in the form of more expensive goods, and in the form of backdoor political deals, which affect our lives just as much.

As with most things, new movements grow from the grass-roots upwards. As more and more people and businesses enact the principles of co-operation rather than competition this will create bridges of positive understanding everywhere and between all people — mutual benefit will be the key to this growth.

Two or more companies (or smaller businesses for that matter) which share their creative resources while retaining their individual integrity can do things which each alone would not be able to do, or would only be able to do after a period of individual expansion, and only maybe at that — depending on the outcome of its efforts.

As more and more companies interact creatively in this way

it will manifest a network — based on the fact that each company represents a number of specialised skills which can be incorporated into a greater whole — for the benefit of that whole, as well as for the benefit of each individual participant.

By extension, in time, businesses will cease to compete, as is the case now, and will mutually assist each other instead. Eventually money (whether cash or electronic money) will be perceived as unnecessary, as it would involve transactions which would no longer be valued as crucial to survival — nevertheless, and obviously, this can only happen when everyone's basic needs are adequately met.

The incentive to work will then no longer be based on anticipated profits, or salaries, but instead it will be based on mutual benefits. Everyone will get what they need; in return everyone will be prepared to contribute to a situation for the sake of benefitting all, including oneself.

This does represent a tremendous evolutionary leap in creative consciousness. There will be those who will resist this evolutionary leap, but they will not be able to prevent this change from occurring — the energies of the New Age, boosted by a global unfoldment of creative consciousness, will favour this leap, and disempower those who favour the old ways of greed, selfishness and status.

Be that as it may, we still have some way to go before we actualise a better world to live in, and there are many issues — including ecological ones — which need to be addressed in earnest. Likewise the plight of the poorer countries and of poorer people everywhere needs to be dealt with in an urgent manner — and this is going to require an enormous effort of creative visualisation to solve.

Even though world resources are not infinite, there is a great need for a radical redistribution of those resources — if we cannot find the answers, then Nature will, and in this case we would have to allow for the fact that the planet is already manifesting its distress by precipitating human negativity back at humans...

We have a very short time to achieve a lot which is necessary and urgently required; and in order to create a new type of civilisation and multi-faceted culture — which will explore space and be able to maintain its coherency, and enjoy its expression — means that each and all of us need to parti*cipate* in that act of creative visualisation, and then act accordingly, and this collectively.

Now!

MEDITATIONS

01 — INTRODUCTION
The best way to start is to get straight into it.

Choose a place where you will be undisturbed; a place where you feel good — free of dust, with access to fresh air (unless that proves to be impractical).

Sit down, comfortably, yet with your spine as upright as possible. Place your hands on your lap, with the palms facing upwards (you can either place the right hand on the left hand, or else separately close to your knees; making a ring between each thumb and index finger is a useful way of *centring* your attention).

Now breathe — a few deep, quick breaths to clear your lungs, followed by gentle, rhythmic breaths; then begin your meditation.

Feel your body filling up with air, and with vitality. As you breathe in, clear your mind of all thoughts, and breathe out any *debris* — including emotions, tension, preoccupations, etc. Go on doing this for 10 to 20 minutes.

For the first week do this each morning and each evening.

It is advisable to *clear* the space around you as well. For this purpose you can think of a bubble of blue light enveloping your whole body; within this bubble of blue light your meditations will take place. It is protective as well; it will also add to your sense of serenity.

During the second week think of the air that you breathe as white light —.breathe it into your body, and feel your body to be filling with more and more light. Gradually lengthen the time of your meditations — up to an hour if you can, or feel so inclined.

If you feel inspired by this simple form of meditation, then you can proceed with the rest of this book. In doing so it is advisable not to race from one kind of meditation to another, but instead to become thoroughly acquainted with each one in turn.

This book is structured in such a way that each meditation becomes more and more potent, revealing pathways towards your Inner Self. To jump ahead — unless you are already well used to meditating — will mean that you will miss out on some of the vital stages which will permit you to make all the *connections* you need to familiarise yourself with in order to access the inner realms of your being, and that of Life — the Higher Planes.

If you feel you need extra information, this book is part of a series which highlights — often in great depth — what is possible, and what you can do in order to enhance your life immeasurably. The other books in this series are: THE PSYCHIC EXPLORER and STARCRAFT.

02 — A MEDITATION PRIMER

While this book or manual in many ways caters for what may be interpreted as fairly advanced stages of meditation, I certainly would not like to feel that newcomers could not either understand or enjoy the information to be found here. Therefore I have introduced this short meditation primer to make things easier for anyone who might feel a bit overwhelmed by the deeper implications involved.

Meditation, from a general point of view, is relatively easy; there is no reason at all to think of it as something that only *fringe* persons might do in an attempt to emulate a yogi, or whoever. In very simple terms, it is a state of inner receptivity; the more inwardly receptive one is, the more one gets benefits from one's meditations.

Conversely, many people assume that meditation is ONLY to be receptive; however, it can be active also: for instance, a business person who is contemplating the ramifications of a business project is meditating after a fashion; s/he is trying to anticipate all the moves which will take that project from a stage of being an idea into a stage of becoming a reality — and there is a lot to think about: the idea itself; its viability; how to manufacture it; how to market it; how to advertise it; where to get raw materials, and so on.

This book does not really deal with that aspect of active meditation (however, its companion book, THE POWER OF CREATIVE VISUALISATION (part of this bundled manual), does). Nevertheless it does impart information with regard to the so-called *occult* use of meditation; *occult* means that which is normally unseen, yet not *unseeable*.

At this point it may be useful to make a certain differentiation between what could be called *mystical meditation, occult meditation,* and *magickal meditation.*

A mystic is someone who views certain inner perspectives of life — however, s/he is a receptor; not an actor. S/he *sees* things; s/he may be a good *channel* for inner impressions; s/he may become something of a prophet/ess; a psychic or clairvoyant — with a more or less definite sense of Spirituality. S/he will not necessarily be religiously inclined, however — in a conventional way at least.

A true mystic is someone who is very clear about what s/he *sees*, and s/he derives a superior, or else highly Spiritual sense of identity from what s/he perceives.

Whenever ego comes into the picture, mysticism becomes degraded, and what is seen is no longer perceived very clearly; it becomes tainted with personality projections; the person involved can become prone to aberrations of all sorts — either in the context of the information s/he gives out, or with regard to how s/he projects hirself ("I am the Only one which the Masters communicate through", and nonsense of that ilk...).

A true occultist, on the other hand, is someone who tries to apply inner knowledge for the sake of getting desired results. S/he may be less intent on being a visionary, and far more concerned with *making things work*. At this level there are two main kinds of occultists: those who try and force things to happen; and those who flow with Life and identify themselves with its currents, and bring about useful effects through right action — often in deep and loving co-operation with creative devas (or the angelic evolution). The former kind of occultists are brash in their activities, and sometimes relatively selfish as well; the latter kind identifies itself with the evolutionary Life-processes, and sees itself as intermeshed with these.

A true magickian is someone who uses magickal methods in order to get occult results, and who needs to be sufficiently receptive and visionary in order to act properly. In other words, a magickian is, ideally at least, the perfect blend of a mystic and an occultist.

This book deals more with magickal meditation.

For the purpose of this primer, let us assume that you know very little if anything about meditation.

One of the first things which you need to take into account is your breathing — for without breath, there is no physical life, at least as we know it, and no power.

Meditation requires a conscious synchronisation of the external and internal *bodies,* or *energy-sheaths;* and deep breathing permits this to be accomplished. Once you realise that each *energy-sheath* represents a certain type of consciousness it becomes easier to understand why the synchronisation of these *bodies* is both necessary and very much a vital part of meditation.

Breathing is a way of *calling* power — one's Kundalini or Shakti (the cosmic energy embedded in the Base chakra); para-chakric energies; Devas; Adepts; archetypes; etc.

Breathing also creates a rhythm, and rhythm is very important when it comes to practising magick (the final *k* is to differentiate magick from stage magic). Magick is essentially a method of *building* power-forms out of life-energies — therefore rhythm and symbolic ceremony are often very useful in magick. Once the power-forms have been constructed it then becomes possible to precipitate them into objective existence, and then use them; and/or to enhance one's consciousness and personal strength.

Since creative devas are the masters of creating power-forms, magick should always be carried forward with their willing assistance; to actually force devas into doing work which they do not care to do is to invoke future, if not immediate, trouble for oneself, and possibly for others. To force Life's natural agents of creative expression against their will is paramount to stupidity.

This is why meditation should not be seen as a sort of suburban pastime for those who have idle moments to spare. Conversely, it is a highly beneficial activity which can bring about untold good results — for the sake of personal liberation; for the sake of world peace and evolutionary growth; for the sake of cosmic *alignment* and unfoldment (more of that later).

If what has been said so far captures your imagination, then read on; if not, then you are probably not yet ready to involve yourself with the true nature of meditation.

03 — BEING IN TUNE

If you were to think of yourself as a television receiver, in order to access a particular channel you would either press a pre-set button designated for that purpose, or you would turn a tuning knob to sample different channels which might be *on air*.

Well, meditation is not all that different from doing this. By entering into a deep state of receptivity, first of all by breathing in a more conscious sort of manner, you then need to *tune in* to the *area* of Life which you want to access — whatever that might be.

Imagine (and this is a fact, although it can be seen in different ways) that you are surrounded by emission sources — TV programmes, if you like. In principle you can tune in to any one of these and thereby perceive the signals inherent to a given broadcast. However, can you tune in to them clearly? Is the screen clear? Is the picture in focus and is it steady? Are the colours right? Is the sound coming through properly as well?... In other words, can you interpret those signals accurately — in a meaningful sequence?

Assuming that you can do so, is the programme worth tuning into? Is it going to bring something into your life that you really need — either by way of information, by way of *feeling*, or by way of identification and energy?

Assuming further that you can discriminate for yourself between what is worth tuning into and what is not, is the range of your receptivity sufficiently extensive to permit you to access programmes which are outside the normal scope of most people's sensitivity?

If not, are you prepared to try and extend your personal range?

If the answer to that is *yes*, then you must be prepared to spend some time, maybe several years at the very least, doing this; if you feel you haven't got that sort of time, then the question must be, "Why not?"

Meditation is an art, and like all arts it must be learnt; and inspiration plays a great part in that learning. As a general rule, an artist — let's say a painter — does not create masterpieces right away; s/he must experiment, and probably learn techniques from others, as well as develop hir own, maybe unique technique, or techniques. The same goes for meditation. From one point of view it can be taught; and from another it is something which you must learn ultimately for yourself, and more or less by yourself — although the *works* of others may well inspire you from time to time... perhaps by pointing out a direction which you had not thought of before; or by imparting the subtlety of a technique which you had not yet devised for yourself.

Getting back to the analogy of a television receiver, once you start to perceive ALL of Life's expressions as sources of information and energy (better yet as information-energies), then you will be in a position to acknowledge the infinite number of broadcasts which are accessible — providing you can enter into the range of their transmissions. This is also tantamount to saying that there is an infinite range of consciousness *positions* to be tuned in to — both within yourself, and without of yourself.

In the end, and above all else, it is consciousness that we are talking about here. To be conscious of something, to whatever extent, is to perceive something of its reality. If you are only partly conscious of it, then you will only see a small part of what it is; if you are very conscious of it, then you can enter into the domain of its reality — in a sense, even if only for a short time, you can *become as it is*.

The more you can do this with fluency and at will, the more you can *align* yourself with all sorts of sources of energy-information — from elements of your own personal psyche to Cosmic Foci of consciousness (the latter are not likely to be your first ports of call, however).

Think about everything which has been said so far — better yet, MEDITATE on it. Breathe it into your consciousness! Enter into rhythmic affinity with it...

04 — SOME SIMPLE MEDITATIONS

Are you sitting comfortably (and don't bother about trying to strain your legs into a lotus position, unless that comes naturally to you)? Then we shall begin.

Imagine yourself to be on a sandy beach. Sunshine is bathing your body with gentle warmth. The sky is clear, and a slight breeze is playing with your hair. Waves are crashing lazily on the shore, and almost reach your feet.

You realise that you are at the confluence of the four primordial elements of fire, air, water and earth — a magickal place to be in. indeed. Around you, and passing through you, there is a fifth element: ether — unseen, but there.

Focus on your Third Eye, or Ajna point — which is slightly above your eye-line, and between your eyes. Feel yourself *breathing* energy in through that point — rhythmically, in and out, in synchronicity with the rhythm of the waves. Breathing in sunlight; breathing in air — moving the watery element within you (the water within your physical body, and the energies of your astral body — i.e., the *energy-sheath* which permits you to be sentient, a creature of feelings and emotions). You are firmly sitting on the sand (representing the earth).

Feel the balance between all these elements — the harmony between them. Feel how the rhythmic breathing soothes all of these elements within you and without of you. Feel the deep peace which you are entering into — and yet also the inner alertness, the clarity, the sense of vital attention.

You feel energised. You feel healthy. You feel joyful at being *in harmony* with all Life.

From this state, go deeper into your meditation. Your Third Eye *opens* up to reveal the ether — the fifth element. Around you, you can now see things which you did not know were there — beautiful things. Your Third Eye can also act like a telescope — you can now see things which are more distant. Have a look around at different things within the *etheric energy-scape*.

Then, in your own time, come back to a state of normal consciousness.

Another simple meditation:

This time you are sitting on top of a mountain peak. The sun is dazzling in its light, and below you can see a vast landscape of mountain ranges and valleys, rivers and trees. Clouds hang over parts of these ranges. You (literally) feel on top of the world — the air is crystal pure; you feel ultra alert. Allow your eyes to wander over what you can see...

The perspective is wonderful — everything seems in such sharp focus. You see a huge bird flying high, and you project your consciousness towards it; you ask it for its permission to fly with it, which it willingly grants if you approach it with love and clarity; you find your consciousness superimposed within its great winged body... It takes you to all sorts of places, which you can see from far above. Then suddenly it plunges at a breathtaking speed towards the ground — do not panic, however. Just enjoy the experience; you are perfectly safe within its care...

It curves towards a valley, and then flies over it — without beating its wings, gliding... Below a silver-coloured river wends its way through the valley; you *fall* out of the bird's body, into the water. Your consciousness becomes superimposed with that of a fish; the fish shows you the mysteries of the river's bed. You feel the water's currents moving around you... how delightful it is to carve your way almost effortlessly through the clear water of the river! Then after a little while you find yourself thrown over the edge of a waterfall, and, airborne, your consciousness flies up into the sky once more. The winged bird intercepts you, and at length takes you back to your body on the mountain top.

Very gently you emerge from your meditation.

A third meditation:

You are sitting by a huge lake; its surface is entirely still. Yet every time that you think, its surface starts to ripple. If you cannot stop yourself thinking, waves start to splash on its shores...

See if you can keep its surface as absolutely still as possible by not thinking a single word, or a single image — except for the lake itself — for the whole duration of ten minutes (or longer, if you feel so inclined).

Feel serene within yourself — so serene that you feel entirely at-one with the lake...

A fourth meditation:

It is sometime just before dawn, and you are walking along a road, which vanishes into the horizon in front of you. It is perfectly straight. Feel your feet walking, yet concentrate the better part of your consciousness on your heart chakra (which projects itself onto your sternum), and focus your eyes on the vanishing point on the horizon...

Then you are walking faster and faster, and you feel lighter and lighter in weight; your feet hardly seem to touch the ground. The road now bends this way, then that. You feel so light in weight now that you are almost a-flight. Then the road is straight once more...

In front of you, you see a great, golden-coloured pyramid, in the middle of an island, surrounded by a lake. The road crosses a bridge onto the island... and now, from behind the pyramid, the Sun rises in all its radiant glory. You find yourself transported to the apex of the pyramid, and then into the centre of the Sun —

in which you feel yourself being charged up with vital energy.

Now you feel strong, and totally in harmony with the Sun and with the whole Solar System; and with your Inner Self.

A fifth meditation:

You are on an unknown world. The terrain in front of and around you is almost entirely flat, and seems hard to the touch. The atmosphere appears to be quite thin — and you can look out into space and see millions of stars, shining very brightly.

Up high you can see the swirl of the centre of the galaxy; you project your consciousness out into space, and go towards that centre. Look at all the stars as you pass them by, at a speed greater than that of light itself... and yet you do not seem to be travelling all that fast, in relative terms.

As you reach the central area of the galaxy you can see a *colony* of central stars — even brighter than all the stars which you have seen so far — and yet their light does not blind you. You enter into the perfect centre — the biggest of all the stars there; pure white — and experience yourself, very gently, and yet also quite powerfully, turning in perfect rhythm with the whole galaxy.

Then you return to the world where you started from, and then to your body on Earth.

(If you find that this meditation has stirred up a lot of energy within you, either meditate on that energy; if you find it *too much*, bathe your face, or even your whole body, in cool, or even cold water; then have something to eat).

CHAPTER 1 — THE PLANETARY ECOSPHERE

Whenever we consider our own lives we must consider also the life of the whole planet. It is a *being* made up of many interrelated parts; and whenever one part is out of harmony with this being (such as the human element), this places stress on all the others.

The following meditations and correlated information are aimed at bringing the human element back into harmonious contact and relationship with the whole planet. Since this cannot be achieved overnight, this process starts with each one of us as an individual; as the process unfolds and includes an ever greater number of individuals, it becomes more and more of a group process; as time goes on it has the potential for becoming a global process.

1 — TREES

Tree are living beings. As soon as one realises and acknowledges that, then trees can become friends in different ways.

Most of us love tree. Certainly our earthly lives depend on them: they provide us with the oxygen we breathe. They also decorate the landscape, thereby making life on Earth that much more pleasant and inspiring.

Anyone who has spent any time looking at trees will have noticed the beautiful variety of shapes, sizes, colouration and expressions that exists. Some people have likened trees to *very slow explosions of energy;* just look at them — it's easy to see them that way.

They also provide homes for birds and certain animals, not to mention insects. We also harvest them (not always in a very caring manner, however) for the wood they can provide us with for making things, or for fire fuel.

And trees increasingly depend on us, because as we are using more and more of the resources that they furnish us with, we are not always sufficiently conscious of THEIR needs. Trees grow slowly; they cannot be replaced overnight; and stripping down the Earth's tree mantle, particularly the rain forests, not only creates almost irreparable damage, it also creates desert-inducing situations, like in Ethiopia, and in turn this threatens our very existence (not to mention that of animals and birds, etc.).

We need to plant more and more trees, everywhere, regardless of any *practical inconvenience* this may create for us. We need to manage arboraceous plantations with understanding and intuition. We need to make sure that all species get a chance to survive and grow.

Tree meditation can put us in touch with the reality of the trees; their lives. Once we have entered into attunement with trees we can also find that they have much to offer us by ways of insights into Life... for in a sense, Life is a Cosmic Tree.

Let us assume that that you know very little about meditation (and if you know more, so much the better). Go somewhere where there are trees; and look for one which you feel particularly good about — one which attracts you... even if you do not really know why.

Go up to it. Put your arms around it; put your forehead on its trunk. *Feel* it.

Allow yourself to be fully sensitive to it. Feel the power arising from its roots, up through its trunk, out into the branches, and the sub-branches, and into its leaves. Feel the sunlight playing on these, photosynthesising the chlorophyll (which consists of carbohydrates formed from the carbon dioxide of the atmosphere and from the hydrogen of water).

Feel this process at work. Feel its life-force. Then try and imagine what it is like to be a tree, from season to season, from year to year, growing, evolving, resonating to its own tree-program. Its leaves and branches swinging back and forth in the wind; a calm radiance on a calm sunshiny day, intaking the radiation from the Sun; shedding worn-out leaves in Autumn; leafless in the dead of winter, with its little buds ready to *explode* forth at the first real sign of sustained Spring.

Now put your back to it, and put your hands backwards against its trunk. Meditate on it. Allow yourself to become at-one with it; and become the tree.

Feel yourself experiencing what the tree experiences; feel its relationship with other trees of its kind, its group tree-soul; feel its relationship with other species of trees; feel its relationship with the ground, from which it derives its nourishment and much of its power; feel the power within the ground; the way that the tree brings this power up above the ground, and how it brings down the sky-power and the sunlight into the ground. The tree is a giant antenna. It picks up cosmic messages; tune into those messages...

Imagine yourself to be within the tree; see the fibrous channels along which the sap rises, and the sky-force descends. Go down into its roots, and dwell there in consciousness, feeling cosy. Feel the warmth of the earth all around you, the peace of the tree; the healing energies...

The surrounding earth seems black; there seems to be no light. Then suddenly you realise that the earth is alive with energy, coming in from all directions: the tree has created a whirlpool of attraction by virtue of its existence — there, at that spot. The earth is full of colours...

Allow images to come to you — they may reveal unsuspected mysteries — of the tree-soul; of your soul... Allow the tree to be your guardian; the tree will protect you (providing you are in harmony with it).

Then, after a while, go up through the roots into the trunk once more, and move further up into its branches, and then its end-extremities... As you do so, think of this as an ascent into the Heavens. You may well get a glimpse of other Planes of Existence, i.e., other Levels of Being... all superimposed in the same space, and also in other spaces. Then at last you may perceive something of the Mysteries of the Trees, of Nature, and of its esoteric counterpart, Super-Nature.

Different trees can help you have different sorts of meditations. Meditating on or with a pine will be quite different to meditating on or with an oak; the pine favours a relatively quick growth, and straightforwardly bursts upwards into the sky; its essence aims at being dominant; as it sheds its needles these create an acidic soil, and as it shoots upwards to reach the sunlight, along with other pines, it impedes that light from reaching the ground — this prevents most other plants from growing in the same area; pines are not the most social of trees; they like keeping to themselves — nevertheless they are very communal and gregarious amongst themselves; whereas the oak gnarls itself into existence, twists and even spirals over water spots... It allows *parasites* to grow on it, more so than pines do. It has a feeling of age; of ancestry; of a strange sort of wisdom. Whereas pines are about power — particularly the beautiful giant redwoods; oaks are about endurance and time.

Tuning in to a beech tree is quite different; the beech tree is sensuous; it evokes sexuality. It *feels* very feminine; sometimes alluring, sometimes poetic... In old age it is like a powerful Matriarch, although, unfortunately, beech trees do not spread their roots quite laterally enough, and they often fall over. Nevertheless, whenever they manage to grow to an old age they are extremely impressive in their power.

A birch is different yet; it *tinkles*; and a willow sings over a stream or river — sometimes a lazy, uncontinuous song...

Each kind of tree has its own mysteries, its own qualities, its own particular soul-essence.

If you care to spend some time meditating on or with different trees, you will find that they have all sorts of things to teach you. Different *modes* of expression; different sensitivities... Different strengths... Things about the past... And all these can become your sensitivities and strengths as you learn from the trees — in meditation.

2 — EARTH

Our planet is a relatively small one, and yet it harbours life quite luxuriantly. The heat derived from the interaction of the atmosphere and the Sun's light is temperate enough for carbon-based cellular-existence. The Earth accumulates this heat during the day, and gives it back to the atmosphere at night. It also has its own heat, coming up from its centre, created by the pressure on the metallic matter to be found at its core.

Here and there power-spots are to be found; some are obvious, because in ancient times the ancient people of the lands erected stone edifices to mark, and then *work* these spots magickally (many Christian churches are built on the sites of more ancient Pagan stone circles, or henges); others are not so obvious — perhaps because they are smaller in power, or because they are relatively inaccessible. Up in the mountains they can be immensely powerful. Others can be found in caves; near waterfalls; in forests....

Some power-spots are *huge:* Stonehenge, Avebury, Glastonbury, Iona (UK), Mt. Shasta, Mt. Taylor, Grand Teton (USA), Machu Pichu (Peru), Everest, Annapurna, Kanchenjunga (Himalayas), Ayers Rock (Australia), the Cheops Pyramid (Egypt), Kilimanjero (Tanzania), Mont Blanc (France), and there are many, many more. Some of these are relatively dormant at present (Avebury, for instance); some are *alive*; some are in high places (mountains especially); and some are in the low lands; some are even below the oceans.

Many large cities are also built on power spots, including London, Los Angeles, Delhi, for instance — cities are invariably *centres of power* around which humans aggregate, often without knowing why. Each centre has its deva; each smaller spot has its lesser deva.

All the power centres and power spots of the Earth are interconnected — by power-leys; this creates a matrix of energy lines right around the planet. There are major power-leys, intermediate ones, and lesser ones — a different sort of *tree-*

system, in fact; all straight lines of contact. Some energy lines undulate, however — their power is more subtle (you could say more *female*), and yet they can be just as powerful in their own way — if in a different manner.

Some harbour an uprise of electro-magnetic energies which can disrupt a compass' needle; some are whirlpools of relatively unknown forces. And all this is somewhere around you — for wherever you are and wherever you may go, you will find power spots, power lines, etc.

Certain types of power-centres may be more remote, more isolated, or more inaccessible, yet even these can be *known* — either (and especially) by going there to meditate, or by tuning into them from a distance — particularly if where you are standing is on a power-line which goes through that centre.

Let us assume that you know of a power-spot with which you feel an affinity. Go there, and sit down (or remain standing; there is a good case for doing different things in different places). Allow yourself to become sensitive to the power which is there; once you feel it, then become part of the power surge, and allow your energies and consciousness to be *moved* by soaking up some of the power into yourself; let it pervade throughout your whole body (and more precisely, your various bodies: physical, etheric, astral, and mental, and all the psychic and Spiritual layers), and let it charge up your ajna (Third Eye) centre, or chakra; then you may *see* things which are not normally perceived.

Different places are good for charging up different chakras: for instance, some power-spots are full of *heart* — soulful essences, which can stimulate the heart chakra in a very beautiful, sometimes even ecstatic and unitive fashion. Others are good for creative expression, and these alter the frequency of the throat chakra. Others yet have an effect on the emotions, or astral energies (via the solar plexus; negative spots of this kind should be avoided — these exist as well; *feel* and choose your spots in this respect); some are good *vitalisers* (of the etheric body, via the spleen chakra and two centres in the shoulder blades; conversely some have a depleting effect, and these should also be avoided); and some can excite the sexual centres (especially certain power-spots to be found in certain caves) — some of these affect women more so that they will men; and vice-versa.

Most *sacred* power-places (acknowledged as such, or *wild-spots*) will stimulate all the human centres, if they are attuned to in the right fashion.

By tuning into the network of energies which pass along the power-leys and between the power-centres, one can tune into all the power-places throughout the Earth, and even those beyond the Earth — for the most important centres are connected to centres on other planets, and even other stars.

Enough hints for now!?

3 — SKY

The atmosphere around us, particularly the oxygen of the air, is all important to us — and not only for the obvious reason that we need to breathe in order to survive (physically). The atmosphere is a reservoir of vitality; and from a more esoteric point of view it is directly connected with the Mental Plane, and therefore it is also a reservoir of thought-forms and ideas.

Oxygen is a *fiery* gas — i.e., it burns, and it permits the combustion of other materials; it provides us with much of our body heat; it feeds our etheric bodies with vital energy (prana), and animates our physical bodies. As we breathe oxygen into our lungs it combines with atoms of carbon, and we breathe out carbon dioxide; this in turn feeds the photosynthesising plants, which then release oxygen back into the air during the day-time, and keep the carbon.

Nitrogen, which composes about four fifths of the atmosphere, is essential to plant life, and it dilutes the oxygen. In its natural state the atmosphere around the Earth is precisely balanced for the needs of biological (carbon-based) life — which is one good reason for keeping it that way, and avoiding its pollution.

This in itself illustrates the interdependence we have with other life-forms, in this case plants. Just as importantly it highlights the reality of living cycles.

What many people do not realise very consciously is that there is only a very thin layer of air above our heads — above 10,000 feet the oxygen content of the air becomes more rarefied; at 14,000 feet we have great difficulty in breathing (and people unused to high altitudes easily get headaches and start feeling nauseous, because of oxygen deprivation); above 14,000 feet (if not before) we begin to require extra oxygen from an oxygen tank and mask. As soon as we fail to get the oxygen we need our brains start to slow down, our muscles no longer function properly, our hearts beat faster (in order to circulate as much of the available oxygen as possible), our metabolism is upset, the endocrine glands start to malfunction, our lungs have to work much harder... and if the oxygen runs out altogether our bodies can no longer sustain life. Therefore the atmosphere, and especially its oxygen component, is a very precious resource.

In meditation breathing is all essential, because if our physical bodies (and their etheric counterparts) are working well, then we can meditate more deeply, and actually derive power for our meditations from the *prana* or vitality in the air.

We each have several bodies: physical, etheric, astral, mental and Spiritual *bodies*, or *energy-sheaths*; these can be consciously *aligned* in meditation, and consciousness can then travel more readily between the different layers. As one breathes more deeply this has the effect of clearing the blood, which then clears the brain and the rest of the physical body — which can then act as a better channel for subtle energies.

As a result, our astral bodies become still and more receptive, and our minds become more responsive to subtle information-energies, including abstractions, intuition, and direct Spiritual contact.

A simple breathing cycle for meditation purposes is to breathe in for a count of eight, holding on to the breath (without *locking* the lungs) for a count of four, then breathing out for a count of eight; and then keeping the lungs empty (once more without *locking* them) for a count of four, before breathing in again. This cycle should be a flowing, strainless process, and to begin with a very conscious one.

Try it now for a few minutes. Feel your body relaxing as you breathe; feel yourself becoming more and more serene within yourself, and your mind more and more quiescent, and yet alert. Try to avoid thinking words to yourself. After a bit you will find that your consciousness will start to shift and become increasingly responsive to higher energies.

Think of your breath as a wave — going up and down... harmoniously, effortlessly, naturally... Feel yourself entering into ever greater contact with the Life around you; feel your personality self becoming increasingly merged with the higher aspects of your Spiritual Self.

This, in effect, is the basis for all meditation. What else you bring into your meditations is up to you; and the aim behind this book is to inspire you to explore as many different, and yet interrelated, uses of meditation as possible.

Now think of the sky around you (and for the purpose of this meditation being outside in the fresh air is recommended); think of it as an extension of your lungs: as you breathe it, so it breathe you. Your life is intermeshed with the life of the atmosphere.

Think of your ajna point (*Third Eye* — slightly above your eye-line and in the middle of the forehead), and imagine that you are breathing in through that point, and breathing out through your whole body. Breathe in white light and purity, and breathe out any negative energies (including toxins, unwanted bacteria and viruses, negative emotions and negative thoughts); simultaneously, think of your body as surrounded by a blue protective light (see also: 01 — INTRODUCTION).

Feel yourself becoming more and more limpid, lucid, cleaner, and more invigorated. Then bit by bit allow your consciousness to expand into the atmosphere around you, until you have fully become the atmosphere; your consciousness is now fully conscious of ALL the air all around the planet. Continue to breathe in white light, and to surround yourself with blue protective light; breathe in purity, and breathe out impurities — regardless of their sources and levels of toxicity. Then instead of just breathing out the impurities, think of yourself as transmuting them into harmonious, wholesome energies... and by doing this you are helping to clear the air of all the *garbage* which we have surrounded ourselves with, on all levels.

This is an illustration of the power of meditation. The more we do this collectively, the more we can bring about relevant and necessary changes: we are helping, (1) to restore the natural balance of the primary gases in the atmosphere, (2) to transmute negative energies into harmonious ones. The power of the mind is greater than many people think.

This meditation alone could save our planet from further chaos, and encourage everyone to be *in tune* with the eco-atmospheric environment, with Life, and with the Higher Self.

After a meditation of this sort it is important to make sure that no negative energies have been drawn into your aura, or energy-field — this is why it is essential to surround yourself with blue light; it filters out negative energies. If you feel even the slightest hint of pollution within yourself, breathe it out, or better yet transmute it.

Never fear it; just deal with it — gently, lovingly, in a healing way; the idea is to change it in a positive manner, not actually to destroy it.

If you practise this meditation regularly it will then become second-nature to you, and you may be very surprised in how it can change your life very considerably: everything (of a positive nature) will work better for you; you will feel a lot healthier; your body will feel more alive, and you will find it easier to control your emotions and use your mind creatively; good ideas will come to you *out of nowhere*; you will increasingly experience a state of unitive intuition; you will feel *charged up;* you will feel more in touch with Spiritual Reality...

4 — THE HUMAN STATE

A human being is not just a fluke of evolution, which after various experiments, mishaps, and then progress, has arrived at a state of *humanhood*. We are Spiritual beings. Our bodies are vehicles for our spirits during dense incarnation.

Nature provides us with our multi-layered bodies, or energy-sheaths — i.e., there are various grades of devas whose task it is to create these bodies on different levels, as required. If it were not for their efforts and their sustenance we would never be able to live and move around as we do.

But what is all this for? What is the essential purpose of incarnation?

Our spirits are as One — at a Spiritual level, initially, there is no individuality; there is no individual capability either.

In order to create the illusion of possible individuality our higher spirits evolved souls — intermediary agents, if you will — and these souls then started to incarnate fractions of themselves into ever denser energy-matter Planes (which were created for our souls by devas). These layers of density created the appearance of separation, and provided us with a means of establishing our sense of individuality; and then a means of testing our capabilities.

It takes hundreds of lives before we start to make good of the opportunities on offer. Eventually we learn to refine our focus, and perfect it — and the end result is transcendence, when as an individual each one of us merges that individuality with the Cosmic Life.

Life depends for its growth on its ability to generate a great, even infinite, multiplicity of views — and this can only be achieved by creating a process that will generate an infinite amount of individuals capable of enacting and representing that multiplicity of views. Different views can then be merged together as one, and this synthesis then permits Life to see Itself as a multiplicity of beings, while remaining One Single Being in Essence; if those beings are attuned to It, then they can all evolve together, at-One, perfectly consciously — and with a common Purpose at heart.

The whole process of manifestation is a *Cosmic Investment,* of a kind.

Each one of us is a part of Life; each one of us is a part of the Cosmic Being who created Universes for Itself so that It could *grow* — by generating, then assessing and using that infinite multiplicity of views — provided by us as individual parts of It (and by all the other individualised beings to be found throughout the Cosmos — from humans, and other beings who might represent our equivalents elsewhere, to Adepts, right through to planetary, stellar and galactic beings, etc...)

A full consideration of the Reality of this process can become very abstract indeed. Normally we feel time-bound, and space-bound. We interpret the passage of personal experience as a span of time; and yet from a certain, and much higher point of view, we are really timeless beings — in essence. Space, also, from a similar and related point of view, in fact does not exist — it only appears to do so.

Conversely, everything that has ever happened, that is happening now, and that will happen in any future to come, is in fact happening simultaneously in a *momentless moment* — i.e., in Super-Time and Super-Space. Perceived from this angle all manifested life occurs without really occurring; the growth we have mentioned above, in this sense, happens instantaneously — ad infinitum.

When perceived from a slowed-down angle, we sense the passage of time, and we see space — this slowed-down continuum permits us to evolve.

However, this is only a point of view. It is the macro-equivalent of theoretical-to-actual quarks — sub-atomic *particles* which are so infinitely small that in a sense they do not exist — i.e., they flash in and out of existence instantaneously... or so it would seem... And yet in doing so they affect the structural expression of greater sub-atomic particles, and that of whole atoms and molecules — i.e., everything which is manifest, including ourselves as human beings with human bodies; and planets and stars, etc.

Under these circumstances — that of infinite growth attained instantaneously, in Super-Time and Super-Space — consciousness cannot evolve. The leap between infinity-minus and infinity-plus is far too great: the result is no growth in consciousness.

Therefore Timelessness has to be *slowed down* into Time (and more precisely into various types of Time, or the semblance of it). Different layers of energy-density provide the required *resistances*, and in occult circles this process is referred as the principle of Saturn *(The Restrictor)*.

Thus, in one sense, Cosmic Creation — on various levels — could be compared with an electronic circuit board where electricity is manipulated by a microchip and a program, further modified by various electronic and electrical components, and changed or slowed right down by, in this case, resistors, etc..

So we find ourselves conscious of time. However, as soon as we refocus our consciousness *beyond* ordinary life, or beyond what resists our spirits, then we increasingly move towards, or else resume, a state of infinite consciousness, and can thereby acknowledge a living state of Timelessness, or an approximation of it.

As soon as we begin to turn the focus of our consciousness on the inner worlds and the inner states of being, we by-pass what ordinarily restricts our capability for infinite perception. As a result time appears to stretch — a few moments may seem like several hours; and several hours may seem like a moment... Sometimes we may experience both of these effects simultaneously, or even alternately. Time is then seen as subjective rather than actual; its *reality* is somewhat elastic; from this point of view it seems ethereal and arbitrary.

If we stretch time further still, it no longer appears to exist at all; or conversely, it now seems so infinite that the intellect can no longer categorise it using clock-time values. Time becomes aeonic, and then trans-aeonic.

Meditate on all this. Breathe in and out as before, and imagine yourself experiencing each facet of time-reality/illusion as imparted in the paragraphs above. See and feel yourself *in time,* then in *elastic, malleable/variable* time, and finally in timelessness...

Within us (within our subconscious minds) we contain all the experiences we have ever had and accumulated in any and all of our previous times and lives, on various Planes — at an individual level, and at a collective level. By virtue of the nature of infinity we can also enter into affinity with any potential experiences *we have already had in the future.* That is, we can experience our future selves, and derive information from these — at least providing we understand and realise that the information accessed and gained is *only in potential* — i.e., there is an infinity of future alternatives, in potential. Our future selves are our potential selves, and every moment we add to this potential.

By entering into conscious rapport with this potential, with our future selves, and then acting on the information perceived, we establish the actual course of our future.

Likewise, by entering into conscious rapport with our past — especially with that which was creative, positive and of evolutionary significance — we can recall to consciousness abilities which we developed in other times (a recommended book on this is EYE OF THE CENTAUR by Barbara Hand Clow (Llewellyn Publications (USA); 1986; ISBN 0-87542-O95-8); and a good book on *future selves* is the end part of A BRIDGE ACROSS FOREVER by Richard Bach (William Morrow (USA); Pan Books(UK); 1984; ISBN 0-330-29081-9) — see the bibliography at the end of this manual).

We can also access the past psychometrically — i.e., to enter into conscious affinity with information which is embedded subconsciously within ourselves and within our surroundings; energy-matter retains all of its past patterns of development, including those of ambient events, and this for the sake of reference — as does the DNA, which we will consider later.

The ability to access information by psychometric means is something of an art, if not a science; nevertheless anyone can practise psychometry at least to a certain extent, depending on hir psychic sensitivity — however, as an art, it must be cultivated frequently if one is going to derive anything very definite and accurate from this process.

In meditation you can learn to *psychometrise* information from both the past, and even the (potential) future, after a fashion: relax, breathe, clear your mind, shift your conscious focus, and then tune very deeply into your life-essence — as deeply as you can go; then focus your mind on the time, *area,* or object you wish to psychometrise... and allow images to come to the surface of your conscious mind. If you ask question of your subconscious, it will respond — providing those questions are not in any way ambiguous; therefore *clear questions* equal *possible clear answers*. Meditation here means *clear, unbiased mind*. If you allow your conscious mind to *colour* the results, or else to distort the information which is coming up from your subconscious, then what you will perceive will be erroneous — and this in direct proportion to the amount of *coloration* you have injected into the process. Aside from this, psychometry is a very simple attunement process.

However, to obtain good results is demanding: you must obey the *rules* of that process and learn not to interfere consciously, or subconsciously for that matter, with the information which arises from this type of meditation.

If you want to tune into past lives it is often helpful to go to the place where a life may have taken place; and then *feelings* may come to you — for instance, walking around a particular site may bring back subconscious memories of who you were and what you did during a lifetime spent in that environment. Those *feelings* can then become *visions*; and those *visions* can reveal what you then recognise to be *true* — i.e., something/or a life which you had several hundreds, thousands, or maybe even millions of years ago. Alternatively you can tune into a site, or several sites, from a distance.

All the lives you have ever had are accessible; in a sense they are buried within your subconscious. You can draw information from those lives whenever necessary — for instance, a *natural* artist is someone who explored and practised art in another time; in the same way, a *natural* musician will have played music in another life, or even several lives; a psychically *gifted* person is someone who mastered hir psychic abilities to a certain degree in other lives too, etc.

Some of these *natural gifts* are so deeply embedded that they never come up to the conscious surface without conscious effort.

For instance, you may have a feeling for music, but you cannot actually play it. The *feeling* is indicating that inwardly you *know* something about music, yet in your current life you may not have acquired the discipline which makes music-playing a possibility. You do not understand the instrument(s) which you might like to play, and you haven't practised any techniques which would have helped you to come to terms with creating music with that instrument(s). Like all arts, half the requirement is concerned with practising, and the other half is concerned with inspiration (an example of the left-and-right brain syndrome) you may feel inspired, but you haven't got the technique; or you may have the technique, but not the inspiration. Yet if you meditate on the information which you may have accumulated in the past, you can recall both technique and a sense of inspiration; the technique may be different to that which is needed now, yet it can be *transposed* — i.e., you can learn a new technique with regard to playing a different type of musical instrument fairly quickly, because the discipline and sensitivity involved have at least a certain amount of similarity with those you learnt in another life, or lives.

By extension it is possible to transpose one kind of art into another: if you play music well, chances are that you will be capable of adapting the discipline and sense of inspiration required, and learn quickly to write well also. Or create or *invent* things. Or do good business. Or whatever...

By further extension you can transpose your understanding of the present into an understanding of the future, and thus greatly further your understanding of the present — as well as the potential for the future! The more you do this, the more you can bring the future into the present... and then everyone will probably think of you as very trendy and *avant-garde!* Or as a genius. And certainly as *gifted*.

This also has the effect of making your mind very flexible, as well as capable. Providing you acquaint yourself with the information you need at any one time, then practise a discipline which will permit you to use that information creatively, and inspire yourself in meditation also, then you can literally acquire any ability that you want.

This is what we could call the *human state:* our potential is inherently infinite — and this is all the more true once beyond the confines of what could still be considered *human* in nature; we must reach out into the endless evolutionary stream which carries on from there.

There is no final limit; no final goal; no *ultimate* anything.

This can be the basis of many interesting meditations.

5 — DEVA STATE

Devas are the embodiment of energy, and the creators of all manifested natural life-forms. At best we imitate them by making things with the materials which they have provided us. They are our natural complements, in the same way as female and male, or black and white, or green and red are complementaries. They represent the other side of ourselves.

The universes did not come into being arbitrarily; they are not the result of a cosmic accident. They were created. They were created, what is more, by cosmic beings who could materialise principles which were natural — that is, which were inherently simple, however complex these might be in their objective or *externalised* make-up. These beings were Cosmic Devas (i.e., representatives of the female force and life-stream), which acted under the primal impulse which emanated from the male force.

(There is no need to believe this; *see* it for yourself.)

At first the male-polarity essence and its devic complement were merged — there was no separation between the male and female forces; together as one they represented a state of pure androgyny. As things became more and more differentiated, primarily as a result of mental application, the two forces became identifiable as relatively separate.

This means that the devic part of us is as much a part of us as is the human part — even if we do not normally see things from a devic angle; consciously, that is.

Devas see sounds, and hear colours; they focus their consciousness from the outside inwards, whereas we, as human beings, focus our consciousness from the inside outwards. Learning to perceive everything devically, or in reverse, so to speak, presents us with the opportunity to understand what devas actually are; how they live and work; and how we can best relate to them — and then exchange and fulfil our respective needs. This in turn permits us to extend our perceptions well beyond what is normally and humanly possible.

Imagine yourself hearing colours — i.e., the energy wavelengths and interactive alchemy of colours; imagine yourself seeing sounds — including the interactive patterns which different sounds can produce.

Devas have one main preoccupation: creating the forms which life can use for its expression; then maintaining those forms in existence for as long as they are needed. And like us, they evolve — from the tiniest of elementals, through various stages of unfoldment and (devic) responsibility, right up to the MahaDeva, or *Cosmic Mother*.

All manifested life is energy; all energy is devic. Once we have a clear realisation of this we can acknowledge our complete dependence on devas for our existence. As soon as we realise that devas are another *side* of ourselves, then we can enter into a much greater realisation with regard to our total potential as a being — i.e., both devic and human.

A deva does not need a body for hir existence, because s/he is the essence of energies, and the essence of the movement-patterns which different energies represent. S/he *is* energy. Even all grades of matter are energy — in fact they are really different states of electricity. A deva modulates this energy, and derives a sense of identity by expressing it in the first place, then through handling it (literally by expressing hirself, then through handling hir own energy).

... Whereas we derive our sense of identity by expressing ourselves as human beings, including handling the energies and the embodiments which devas provide us with, and thus evolving our sense of consciousness.

Devas *program* natural existence; we deal with the *programs* which they enact. As we unfold our lives, they provide us with our various needs — i.e., the energies and conditions which we require in order to unfold further in our evolutions. Therefore, underneath the surface of things, human-type intelligences and devic beings co-operate to bring about new growth. The more we willingly and consciously co-operate with devas, the more they can provide us with exactly what we need; and we can provide them with what they need — the opportunity to unfold their capabilities further as well, through mutual co-operation.

Once we understand this interdependence between the human and devic states, we can learn to fuse both evolutionary streams.

Meditation: feel the periphery of your body — everything which is happening inside your body is the result of devic energies combining in various ways, in various forms; your whole body is devic energy-matter. Enter into attunement with this energy-matter; then become conscious of all the energy-matter which is immediately outside of your body as well — it is, in essence, the same energy-matter. Expand your consciousness into all the energy-matter which surrounds you throughout the whole planet; the whole solar system; the whole galaxy; the whole universe... You are now (at a consciousness level) the embodiment of all the energy-matter within the whole Cosmos, extending as you do in every direction, ad infinitum.

If you did this perfectly, i.e., with your consciousness fully alert, then you may have experienced Union with the Cosmic Mother, or MahaDeva. This meditation is best done by focusing all your attention on the heart chakra.

Another meditation: go to a place out in nature, and meditate on the natural environment which you can see and otherwise perceive; imagine yourself expanding your consciousness to include all the energy-matter, all the life-forms, and all the devic essences within that environment. Project your consciousness through the blades of grass; enter into the aperture of a flower; dwell in a tree; fly to the highest point within the landscape... remaining conscious at all times of the totality of that environment. Become the landscape; you are an extension of it, and it is now an extension of you.

A third meditation: imagine that you are a deva of a certain planetary type; you are responsible for the formation and the unfoldment of a whole planet (let us say the Earth) — and this in partnership with other devas of the same kind; and you guide lesser creative devas into working out your planetary schemes.

The planet must be built in stages, Plane by Plane. You think of it (Mental Plane); you dream of it (Astral Plane); then you project your *intent* downwards still, into the etheric state, which you create — and finally you see the initial primary energy-matter coalescing itself under your direction into a ball-shaped mass of substances — still very basic and crude; and increasingly dense and physical (physical plane).

Feel yourself channelling vast amounts of energy from extra-planetary sources, and modifying that energy as may be appropriate for your task. Then as the planet starts to take shape, and then solidify, imagine what you would have to do in order to make biological life possible on its surface: creating more and more complex atomic substances — gases, liquids, different kinds of stony materials, metals, crystals; then very basic and very small life-forms — bacteria and viruses which do not need oxygen for their survival; then you create other kinds of bacteria, and as a by-product of their waste these produce methane.

These bacteria multiply and multiply, producing more and more methane; out of the ambient gases you then create storms, and the electrical discharges split water into hydrogen and oxygen, and you create more micro-organisms; then greater life-forms — algae, small plants, then greater plant-forms — which breathe out oxygen. The need for the over-abundance of methane-producing bacteria has come to an end, and the presence of ever-greater amounts of oxygen starts to limit their numbers. The atmosphere, which so far has been very dense and relatively opaque, begins to clear, and sunlight finally gets through.

As we have seen in an earlier section, plants which photosynthesise sunlight release oxygen into the atmosphere (that is, during the day; at night they breathe it instead) — you now have enough of the right sort of gases which will permit an increase in the complexity of carbon-based life-forms; you create ever-bigger plants, and now you have trees... whole jungles in fact. Meanwhile you have created small insects to help with the pollination of the flowers, and an increased yield of plant-forms has resulted; then the insects begin to overwhelm the eco-system developed thus far, so you create other, more complex organisms which will derive nourishment from these insects.

You are forever trying to maintain balance as well as ensure progress. Then you create fish, then small animals out of the earlier prototype life-forms; again balance is necessary, therefore you create even more complex life-forms — including much bigger ones; and these feed themselves on the now prolific amounts of smaller animals and fish; however, these more complex life-forms in turn create an imbalance.

The huge dinosaurs you have created do not appeal to the spirits who want to incarnate anyway — so you bring about a situation which will reduce the dinosaurs in numbers, yet meanwhile some of them have adapted, and have become birds (with your help, of course). You go on creating animals, and from reptiles you pass on to marsupials and mammals; finally, many millions of years later, you arrive at a new prototype, half reptilian, half mammalian: the prototype of the human type which you are trying to conceive of, and which your *clients* — the would-be incarnating spirits — actually require for their evolution.

This prototype is still very gross in its manifestation, yet you keep on refining the form until it becomes more to the liking of the would-be *users* of that form. At length they incarnate, but they find the form too limiting; so you refine it even further, and from an egg-bearing hermaphrodite which reproduces its young by parthenogenesis it becomes a split-sexed mammal — i.e., you have now created male and female types — and this mammal creates its young by diversifying genetic material through sexual intercourse.

You increase its brain capacity, and it begins to think for itself, albeit only in a very rudimentary fashion. This time your *clients* are somewhat more impressed, but they want more — for this *animal* is still far too unconscious, and far too limited in its capabilities. It has telepathic abilities, but no real sense of individuality.

You call on a cosmic being (from Sirius, was it?!) to initiate a greater sense of individuality, and you give your creations the capacity for increased individualised thought... knowing full well that there is a risk involved in this, but knowing equally well that it is necessary (the prototype for the myth of Eve and Adam, and the infamous *apple,* is born).

These creations are progressively losing their sense of Oneness with the Cosmic Being because they are becoming more and more self-oriented. Later in time, although you have further refined the human types, they have engrossed themselves meanwhile in schisms, have warred amongst themselves, have experimented in all sorts of directions, and have, as a result, created all sorts of imbalances.

To save the planet from destruction at their hands you adjust the frequency sensitivity of the energy-substances within the planetary environment, and then oversee several great earth movements and oceanic floods — these are the results of human wrong-doing, yet they are truly devastating in their effects; nevertheless, above all else you must make sure that the planet itself survives. These *catastrophes* reduce human civilisations back to an early stage of regrowth.

You know full well that no one has really *died;* the spirits of the human egos which have lost their physical bodies during these events will only reincarnate again, and again — until they finally learn to be at peace with each other, and to re-attune themselves with the Cosmic Being.

Yet humans persist in their folly from era to era — they go on warring amongst themselves, and go on creating the means of inflicting injury, dominance and death — not to mention many other atrocities.

Acting jointly with human Adepts — i.e., those who managed to emerge transcendent from the turmoil *below* — you continue to bring about circumstances and situations which will help human beings to realise that they could derive a lot more benefit from mutual co-operation through positive relationship... yet only a few are genuinely responsive. Time passes by, and a new dominant civilisation has now produced a multitude of weapons with which to annihilate a potential aggressor of its own species — and thereby, once more, possibly annihilate the Earth in the process.

Therefore you look out for those who can use their minds more creatively, and you inspire them to balance out this situation. They see what is needed, and they start to network their thoughts using the media at their disposal, and then begin to experience various states of telepathic rapport between themselves; and with other beings, including yourself and your devic representatives. In fact — with your help — they learn to meditate so deeply that they effectively help to induce a mental atmosphere which forces the rest of the species — via politicians wherever possible — into making arrangements so that nuclear war is averted; those who make these decisions then consolidate on the arrangements made and decide for the first time to co-operate in a global attitude of sharing and mutual benefit.

At last you have created a truly intelligent and responsive human type, which can now see the way ahead — living in harmony with itself, and with the Cosmos at large...

(The above meditation is not designed to take all the evolutionary steps into consideration — nor is it exactly representative of what really happened, or is happening now).

6 — FUSION STATE

The whole process of manifested life on this planet (and it is essentially analogous everywhere) is a co-creation. The inner parts of our being create the outer worlds for our outer selves; through experience our outer selves develop individuality and abilities, and then rediscover mutuality with the Spirit.

Once Life is *seen* and acknowledged in this way it removes the need for any ill-defined concepts of religion. Perception in itself is not a religion; at best *religion* means *to be re-linked with,* but if that turns out to be some mysteriously punitive god, that is pure and simply a human aberration; or a way of manipulating people's fears.

Sexist terms must be transcended, therefore we cannot talk of a *God* without talking of a *Goddess*; however, this indicates lower Planes duality. On a Spiritual Plane there can only be *Goddess*, even if one side of that Androgynous Essence is treated as female, and the other side as male (or of devic and human-type).

On an individual level this applies as well: within us there is a deva; on the outside there is a human being. Put the two together — because in fact they are already together, intrinsically, even if the human part fails to acknowledge this and you have the perfect being; the perfect *you*. Become at-one with your deva (or Solar Deva; Solar Angel), and your deva will become at-one with you — allowing dual, merged perception — human and devic.

Once you have done this fully, you *know*; you *see*; you *hear*; you *feel*.

The ancient Tibetans acknowledged this, and this is why perhaps, (1) they did most things in reverse to the way we do them, (2) they started with the most Cosmic Concept they were capable of perceiving, and went all the way down into the outer details — i.e., the opposite of what we usually do; we put a lot of details together, and then try and conclude, synthetically, with a huge Concept, or an all-embracing Theory — a *punch line;* but the Tibetans actually started with the *punch line!*

Meditate on your (Solar) deva, and on all the perception reversals hinted at previously. Once you have *seen* from a devic point of view (we'll assume here that you can), then merge that completely with your own human point of view. If you manage to fuse the human and the deva aspects of yourself into *one single* consciousness, then you can then consider yourself something of an Adept (that is, providing you can sustain this state of consciousness at will).

This is to make it sound easy — it isn't. The initial contact with your deva can be a most powerful one; and s/he may present hirself to you as male if you are a woman, and as female if you are a man.

Why is this?

Because this appears to be a device for attracting your attention. Your deva knows just how easy it is for you to lose your focus of higher consciousness, assuming that you have attained anything of significance in that department in the first place. Increased conscious interaction with your deva will draw you increasingly into a sort of psychic trans-sexuality... until you self-realise yourself as a fully conscious, androgynous being.

Your deva will come to you in various ways: in your visions; in your dreams; during your out-of-the-body projections (see THE PSYCHIC EXPLORER); during moments of altered states of consciousness; in your meditations... in channelling...

S/he will also come to you in less obvious ways: organising things for you in the background; testing you; playing games with you... unless you become humourous enough, and insightful enough, to know what s/he is really up to... and even then...

Once the fusion takes place (and this is a progressive event over a period of years, with peaks at intervals), you will eventually experience great joy and fulfilment — because you will have rejoined with your essential, natural, fully androgynous state of being.

7 — SUPER-NATURE

The Higher Planes; Super-Nature; call it what you will... It may seem somewhat abstract (at first), yet it is perfectly real — in fact it is *dynamically real*. In other words, its potency is far greater than anything we experience normally; and nature as we know it can be viewed as an extension of it. Conversely, Super-Nature represents various interrelated *Zones of consciousness* where *super-natural* events take place; in effect, it is your natural habitat at a Spiritual level.

Imagine a *landscape* full of coloured energies — radiant, prismatic, dynamic, electric, magnetic, and very potent. Call it a partially merged perception of various levels of existence — representing the world that sorcerer/esses explore in earnest in order to find their freedom and sharpen their abilities.

As a meditator you may elect to remain comfortably at home in your armchair, meditating away; alternatively, and this can only be recommended as a far superior course of action, you could be walking around nature close to an ancient power-site, or sitting on a power-spot — however, in one sense it doesn't really matter where you are physically, because space is illusionary; and when your deva is present (in your consciousness) you will be afforded plenty of support by way of power and insights.

Yet in another sense it does matter, because the power at a power-site can lend energy to your inner perception of things. A great grouping of people all delving into their inner Selves acting in one place makes that area a power-site, after a fashion; yet if they are actually located at a power-site, then their experiences can be quite revealing.

Systems of magick have evolved from a need to co-ordinate energy-streams (devic energy-streams) in order to get a result. For instance, Shamanism attempts to flow with the forces of Super-Nature; so does genuine Witchcraft, or Starcraft; the so-called Western Tradition, based on the Jewish Kabbalah (therefore Middle Eastern), attempts to force energy-streams into a desired result. Many Eastern techniques attempt to negate Nature altogether in favour of abstractions.

Devas do not like to be forced; yet they will co-operate with humans. Magick is a method of co-working energies, from one angle; it is a state of consciousness, from another. A sufficiently high consciousness, merged with the use of a vital method, can produce excellent results: psychically-spiritually, conceptually, and practically.

In essence, and for the most part in practice, there is a great difference between a Magickal group and a religious group. Magick is pragmatic, even when the concepts it uses for its *triggering* are sometimes highly abstract, yet still natural. A religious group, however, is often, and at best, practising emotional magick; or emotional games (which it may attempt to inflict on others on occasions — usually with dire consequences).

It is possible to merge the two, as some do. Nevertheless Shamanism, or true sorcery (or Sourcery), is not about worship, or devotion, or arbitrary rituals — it is about perceiving and about learning how to shift the focus of one's consciousness, and through altered perception learning how to be free.

Super-Nature is our heritage — as cosmic beings. The whole point about meditation is to bring about cosmic consciousness.

There are various ways of interpreting the Cosmic environment. One of the clearest *maps* we have is derived from Tibetan sources, and this defines Super-Nature as a system of Planes.

While overall, Super-Nature can be viewed as a *spectrum* of energies, or as a continuum, the Tibetan view is that there are seven Planes — or seven distinct *zones* of energy, each zone being a function of a certain range of energy or atomic frequencies. The higher the frequency, the higher the Plane.

While all the Planes can be seen as interrelated, each Plane has its own internal *laws*, and thereby represents a specific state of consciousness. The lowest of the Planes is the etheric-physical plane, which the Tibetans do not regard as a principle, but only as the end-result of the process of concretisation of energies into dense forms (which is why this plane is spelt without a capital *P*). This plane accounts for dense minerals, liquids and gases, and for those energies which are often referred to as plasmic or plasmatic, including sounds, physical light, magnetism, electricity, atomic energy, etc.

The Astral Plane's energies are of a higher frequency range, while the Mental Plane's energies are higher yet; the Higher Mental Plane is the 3rd Spiritual Aspect — while the Buddhic Plane is the 2nd, and the Atm(a)ic Plane is the 1st. These three collectively are differentiations of the Monad (Higher Self, resident on the Monadic Plane). Finally there is a Systemic Plane (Adi in Sanskrit), and all seven Planes form the lowest of the Seven Cosmic Planes.

This is how the ancient Tibetans *saw* and interpreted these things; there are other ways of interpreting them, however.

INTERLUDE 1

In THE PLANETARY ECOSPHERE chapter we have covered a few (only a few) of the more fundamental aspects of our planetary life. If you use the meditations often enough you will find yourself becoming more and more sensitive to the planet as a living entity.

Mother Earth.

Of course the Earth is both male and female. However, it is interesting to note from esoteric sources that the Earth is referred to as a sister-planet to Venus; that the Earth and Venus are considered arcanely as one single being, split into two planets, as it were.

Greek and Roman mythologies, amongst others, and astrology, lead us to think of Venus as the planet of love; of relationship; and Venus, as Aphrodite — the foam-born one, is represented as female. Again from an esoteric point of view, Venus is said to express a particular energy unfoldment which, in effect, produces a great clarity of insight, leading to a great clarity of expression. Esoterically it is associated with the Higher Mind, or the Third Aspect of Spirit.

Also it is said that Venus is one evolutionary cycle in advance of that of the Earth — therefore placing Venus in a position of guardianship over the Earth's evolution.

If the Earth was to be thought of as a personality, then Venus, in some ways, would represent hir soul.

According to Theosophy (itself derived from Tibetan sources), the Lords of the Flame *from Venus came to the Earth over 18 million years ago to assist the Earth in hir evolution. The notion of* Lords *is undoubtedly antiquated, and we are not the wiser with regard to their true sexual gender; nevertheless, we are talking about Spiritual beings who had already achieved a great deal by way of personal and group evolution, placing them well above the evolution of humanity even today.*

These beings are also referred to as the Kumaras, with Sanat Kumara as their leader.

Taking this information as a basis for further meditation, we can tune our consciousness into the planet Venus, as an evolutionary being. If Venus in some way represents the soul element with regard to the Earth, then meditating on Venus might well help us to harmonise our conscious expression and understanding to the extent that we may begin to experience soul consciousness.

CHAPTER 2 — THE SOLAR SYSTEM

8 — VENUS

Astronomically, Venus is a planet of roughly the same size as that of the Earth. It is closer to the Sun, which it orbits every 224.7 days. During inferior conjunctions it is also the closest physical planet to the Earth — 40 million miles away — and it can often be seen as a relatively large and luminous point of light against the background of stars.

In the Northern Hemisphere it is often the first *star* to be seen after sunset, and it sets early itself Or rises early, before the Sun, depending on where it is in the sky in relation to the Earth at any one time.

It is covered by a dense layer of clouds, which makes it impossible for us to see its surface characteristics even when using a powerful telescope. By 1950 it was realised that Venus was not the *jungle planet* it was previously thought to be; in fact early microwave measurements revealed that its surface temperature must be very hot — in the hundreds of degrees centigrade. This was confirmed by NASA's Mariner 2 space probe (1973), and further verified by the Soviets' Venera 9 and 10, which landed on the planet (on October 22nd and 25th, 1975, respectively) — safely relaying video pictures and other data to the Earth before they were overcome by the acidity in Venus' crushing atmosphere — about 100 times denser than that of the Earth.

The Venera 9 landing site showed a landscape of boulders strewn across a rocky landscape, whereas Venera 10, which landed 2500 kilometres away, showed a flat, basalt-like surface, with a low outcropping of rock.

At both sites, instruments revealed an abundance of background radioactivity: uranium, thorium and potassium — in other words, elements which are found in volcanic areas on Earth.

Of course this information in itself does not tells all that much about the overall features to be found in the Venusian environment — it would be much like two probes landing on Earth, one in the Arizona desert, and the other on a volcanic island — i.e., giving us only two views out of millions of possibilities. What it does bring to mind is to question how any beings which came from, or still inhabit Venus, could possibly survive on such an inhospitable world.

But then the Kumaras/Lords of the Flame were not necessarily physical.

This remains a question which will need to be answered one day, no doubt. However, esoteric sources tell us that the Venusian stream of human-like evolution is no longer to be found on the denser physical plane; and to be fair, this information antidates the landing of the NASA and Soviet probes by thousands of years. The implication is that the Venusian life-stream transcended its physical environment some time ago.

Assuming that this esoteric information is in any way accurate — such as Venus representing the soul aspect of the Earth's personality — let us evolve the following meditation:

Think of Venus as a planetary entity which has not only transcended much of what the Earth is still experiencing, but which has also a special relationship with our planet. In effect, it is acting as an evolutionary prototype at the Spiritual level.

Let us enter into affinity with Venus — and try and see what we can derive from our meditations on that planet.

Imagine yourself to be on its surface — yet the physical landscape is not what interests us here — we want to *feel* its more subtle energies, its aura, if you like. Allow yourself to be charged up by its energy, and then see what this energy tells you: what effect does it have on your consciousness?

Does it feel powerful? Does it make you feel clearer within yourself? Does it impart any special information about anything in particular?

Does it inspire you? Does it make you feel more *scientific?* Does it make you feel more artistic? More religious? More visionary?...

Scan through these possible effects: power, revelation, creativity, harmony, analysis, emotions, magick... Does any one of these predominate? Do several affect you, and to what degree?... After your meditation (or even during, if you are flexible enough) make as many notes as you can about your impressions; do this each time you have ended a meditation on Venus — after a while you may have a large body of written impressions, which may reveal much of interest to you.

This meditation exercise, bit by bit, will permit you to become more and more sensitive to the evolution of the Venusian life-stream; and eventually you may form a bond of affinity which will permit you to enter into closer contact with it whenever you may feel the need to do this.

9 — THE PLANETS OF THE SOLAR SYSTEM

Of course, you can do the same thing with regard to all the other planets in the Solar System. At length you will have an even greater body of impressions, representing planetary characteristic in consciousness terms. Each planetary source of impressions and energies will then give you extra magickal *tools* to work with.

Finally you will be in a position not only to compare different impressions from different places, you will be able to meditate on the fusion of two or more planetary life-streams — thereby deriving *synthetic* or composite impressions. In essence, this is the basis of astrological sensitivity (as distinct from the traditional notions which surround these planets, most of which notions are somewhat archaic or medieval in character); how do two or more aspected planets influence you, especially when you enter into ever more conscious alignment with them?

How do they affect the Earth as a whole? How does the Earth affect them?

If you have, or get hold of, a good astronomical book of ephemerides (such as THE AMERICAN EPHEMERIDES FOR THE 20TH CENTURY by Neil F. Michelsen (ACS Publications; ISBN 0-917086-19-8), you will be able to plan when your meditations are likely to be the most effective — for instance, when a planet is in trine aspect to the Earth; or when two planets are in opposition; and especially if a situation exists where several planets are all aspected to each other in various ways.

What must be said here is that there is no such thing as an *evil* astrological aspect; the notion that a given aspect (square, opposition, etc.) has an intrinsically detrimental effect is absolutely rubbish — it only indicates a period of extra tension or difficulty; whereas a so-called *good* aspect only indicates a period of greater harmonisation of energies. The latter type of aspect may be less demanding, nevertheless it will rarely provoke any radical changes; whereas the more difficult aspects can sometimes, in fact, precipitate great, and very necessary and worthwhile changes.

It is not the purpose of this book to delve at any length into the mysteries of astrological events and their effects upon us, however there are plenty of books around which deal with astrology adequately enough (even if they only *scratch the surface of things* — there is a lot more to astrology than what is presently understood), and these may well inspire you to become more acquainted with the *eco-relationships* between the planets in this Solar System.

Having said that, this manual is designed to save you a lot of money and frustration reading dozens if not hundreds of books by helping you to tune into any source of information-energies you may care to select for the purposes of your meditations. Why indeed read about what you can learn to access yourself in a direct fashion? Also, whatever has been written by others only outlines their own impressions — which may not be accurate, or even terribly relevant.

Be original. Be daring. Go and inquire about the universe yourself, i.e., do it first hand — do not leave it to others to do this for you.

Once you have mastered the essential methods of meditating you can turn your inner *gaze* to anywhere you care to look and *see*, and *feel*. You can enter into a vast number of different relationships with different places and different beings — particularly highly evolved beings. At first these may not be able to communicate with you very straightforwardly because of your own limitations; nevertheless as you enlarge on your *area* of contact and become more fluent with your meditational skills you will be able to derive all sorts of impressions which you may find not only of great personal interest, but also of great personal use.

Again, we are dealing here mostly with consciousness, rather than with nut-and-bolts facts. The purpose of meditation is to permit you to elevate your sensitivity towards untold heights, until you find yourself in a position to integrate all the energies with which you have, in some manner, become *aligned*. Their effect upon you will then determine how you *feel* and how you *see* life in general, and in the specific; and in consequence your life will change — because you will be living according to new perspectives, and drawing upon hitherto unknown energies — both consciously and subconsciously.

10 — THE SUN

The Sun is a star (many people do not even seem to realise this very clearly!). As far as stars go it is neither the biggest or the most luminous — Antares, for instance, has a diameter 300 times that of the Sun; and some stars output hundreds of times more light than the Sun does (which in itself is the equivalent of the combined light of 136,000 candles seen from a distance of one metre).

While the temperatures within the Sun's core rise to millions of degrees Kelvin, its average surface temperature is about 6000 degrees. Some stars, however, have a surface temperature of 50,000 degrees or more (type *W* stars), while others have a surface temperature of only 3500 degrees or less (types *M*, *RN* and *S*). Therefore in astronomical terms the Sun is by no means either spectacular, or even particularly unique. In fact the Sun is of a type known as *G*, which type includes a very large number of stars in this galaxy.

In Spiritual or esoteric terms, however, the Sun represents a stellar being which has a definite place and evolutionary function within a family of stars, which includes Sirius A, and its dense companion, Sirius B (approximately 9 light-years distant from us).

The Sun *keys in* all the evolutionary developments within the whole Solar System, although other stars and constellations have their individual and group affinities with specific planets within this system. If you want to explore this in a lot more depth, ESOTERIC ASTROLOGY by Alice A. Bailey (Lucis Press), is by far the most comprehensive of information sources in print with regard to the esoteric connections between certain stars and the planets of this Solar System.

That ancient people should have considered the Sun as a god is by no means superfluous to our understanding of Life — indeed, within a certain context, the Sun is indeed a god, or goddess, or god-dess, i.e., a being of an evolutionary status far in advance of ours. Nevertheless, we all have our special affinity with the Sun, since s/he is the cosmic being within whose *systemic body* we are presently living.

From one point of view each one of us is a small *fragment of sunlight;* or in a similar vein, each one of us is a small fragment of hir being.

Meditating on the Sun can be a most beautiful and rewarding experience; furthermore, identifying oneself with the Sun can bring about a revolutionary perception of the Sun's place within the local portion of the Cosmic Network (more on this can be found in JOURNEYING — A WAY OF SELF-DISCOVERY, at the end of this bundled manual); and by implication, since we are directly related to the Sun, we can begin to perceive our own role and purpose as evolutionary beings within a superior evolutionary system.

Imagine yourself lifting off the surface of the Earth, and going towards the Sun. See it becoming larger and larger in your mind's eye, until you are only a little distance away... It's huge; its horizon, as you get closer still, appears to be almost flat.

Land on its surface, then move inwardly into its luminous mass — until you find an *area* where you feel entirely comfortable — i.e., which is neither too powerful, or too intangible. See and feel all the sunlight around you, and then identify yourself totally with the Sun's energies. Become the sunlight; become *as of the Sun;* allow yourself to *be* the Sun — in total harmony with this beautiful cosmic being.

Then try and feel the connections that you may have with other stars — receiving information-energies from other stellar sources, and in turn outputting information-energies to these, or to others, and to the planets within the Solar System; try and *see* what is going on within the Solar System, from the vantage point of the Sun's consciousness.

Obviously, you will only be able to do this to a small extent, at best — a complete fusion of your consciousness with that of the Sun would *explode* your human nature; nevertheless you can practise this sort of meditation in perfect safety, providing your attitude is right; providing you put yourself in a position of genuine alignment with the Sun; providing you go to hir with love and respect; and providing you do not bring your human problems in there with you — i.e., negative thoughts or feelings are intrinsically *not on*.

Then meditate on all the ways you could enter into a creative rapport with the Sun, and by extension with the Solar System as a whole.

INTERLUDE 2

"What is a being like you doing in a place like this?" — this might well be the sort of question that you might find very difficult to answer directly and concisely, because few of us can remember anything much about our past-life and inter-life history. Why, indeed, are you incarnated here on Earth presently?!

At this point we need to remind ourselves of the old arcane adage: *"As above, so below"*.

Whatever we do here, on Earth during incarnation, each one of us in our own individual way and according to whatever it is which is driving us along, is preparing us for what we will do and what we will be in the future — in incarnation, out of incarnation, and beyond the end of our incarnational cycles as well (i.e., once we have transcended the lower Planes).

Whatever we do here in a little way — providing it is evolutionarily creative — will become magnified to the nth degree as soon as we lift ourselves beyond the need to incarnate (by mastering our lower personality natures, and then moving our consciousness into other, much higher states).

From another point of view, whatever it is each one of us is doing here while in incarnation is being paralleled by the more powerful activities of one's Higher Self at a much higher Level — and that higher activity bears a direct symbolic-to-actual relationship to what each one of us is doing as a human being.

Each little victory on Earth is a much greater victory in (the) Heaven(s).

Each difficulty each one of us encounters on the physical plane is a part of a greater difficulty which one's Higher Self is trying to overcome, or else a part of a scheme which needs resolution on other levels.

Seen in this light one's life becomes a good deal more significant — whatever it is that each one of us is doing has a purpose, even if it is only by way of leading the little self into a more *appropriate area of activity which is more conducive to the needs of the Higher Self within.*

Seeing oneself as a multi-levelled being is not easy; whereas becoming engrossed with one's ego identity is quite easy indeed. Understanding the Higher Self is almost impossible for us — until we are initiated into its Reality.

CHAPTER 3 — THE HIGHER SELF

11 — *THE MASTER-SELF WITHIN*

Many esoteric books — especially some of the older ones — speak of the *Masters* as beings who have allegedly perfected their natures to such a high extent that they have, in effect, transcended the limitations of their lower selves; meaning that many of them have departed permanently into the Beyond, while a few maybe have remained around in order to help those not yet liberated from the trammels of lower existence.

Here's another old esoteric adage which you may recognise: "The Master appears when the disciple is ready"; what they do not say is that the *Master* in question is within you!

It is often a humorous moment when one recognises that internal *Master* during a period of heightened consciousness — staring at you, and smiling in the mirror!... and s/he is so obvious, as well.

Another adage: "When the disciple builds one third of the bridge between hirself and hir Master, the Master then builds the other two-thirds."

Build one third of the contact, and your Higher Self will do the rest.

Nevertheless, what does this *bridge* actually consist of?

From one angle it is one of consciousness; from another it is the raising of the Kundalini/Shakti energy embedded within the base of the spine into the head centres, or head chakras; and from another angle yet it is the building of the energy-bridge between a small centre at the base of the skull, and the Alta Major, another centre which can be found just above where the spine joins the skull. When this has occurred, energy-strand by energy-strand, then the *disciple* will have built one-third of the consciousness bridge between hirself and hir Higher Self. Higher energies then circulate freely between all the centres...

... And s/he will recognise hir Higher Self in that moment.

But what is the Higher Self really like? In what way does s/he differ from the lower, personality self?

Imagine for a moment what it would be like to be a cosmic being — in touch with the Cosmic Network, living in an *area* or Level of Life where there are no forms — only patterns of high energy. By virtue of this contact with the Cosmic Network, information is accessible to you at will; any energy which is required can be *obtained* instantly by keying into its source, using your faculty for cosmic intuition and cosmic insight; your sense of consciousness then includes the Cosmic View of the Self.

You *know* that your essential Self has *been around* for hundreds, thousands, or an incalculable number of years — in fact to you the notion of a *year* is a remarkably small fraction of time; even a hundred years seems like a moment; while a thousand years is like an afternoon's reverie; a million years might just seem like a day; your sense of time is aeonic.

You perceive several Layers of Life simultaneously, and you can travel in your consciousness between these Layers at will. You are engaged in cosmic work...

For a moment let us imagine what the Higher Self would see of the little personality self, should it care to *look in* on it: a tiny fragment of its essence which is spending a lot of its own time doing probably very little.

It is because the Higher Self can scarcely relate to what the *little self* is doing that the soul exists; the soul, which lives on hir own level (the higher parts of the Mental Plane, and in some advanced cases on the Buddhic, or 4th Plane), oversees what the little personality self is doing — yet even the soul scarcely preoccupies hirself with what the little self is up to during the early cycles of physical incarnation. S/he has to wait until enough natural development has taken place to make it relevant for hir to actually start *modelling* the lives of the diminutive incarnated portion of hirself; and the soul is only one out of many fragments of the Higher Self.

Whenever the little self begins, at last — after hundreds of incarnations — to respond positively to the soul, the soul then increases hir energy input into the lower self; and as a result the personality self starts to become more responsive and energetic in hir activities.

By the time initiation takes place, the soul starts to become absorbed back into the Higher Self (Monad); and the lower self then encounters that Higher Self at a conscious level (see INITIATIONS, TRANSMUTATION & IMMORTALITY, part of THE PSYCHIC EXPLORER).

Let us make an analogy: during the early period of individualised expression the little self is like a grain of sand when compared with the boulder which the soul is; which in turn looks up at an enormous mountain which towers beyond the canopy of clouds and reaches out into the heavens, representing the Higher Self.

Later, when the lower self becomes somewhat more conscious of the soul, it is still confronted by the enormity of the mountain/Higher Self above — with its steep slopes reaching into foreverness; nevertheless, it has begun to learn how to climb the mountain, and it does so with ever more agility and purpose.

By the time the lower self has attained the first genuine degree of Life Initiation, at least now s/he has met hir Higher Self *face to face*, and has reached one of the first of many high peaks. The mountain still appears to be vast, but no longer seems quite so *inconquerable*.

At the advent of the third Life-Initiation — when the individualised self becomes, technically, a *Master*, and s/he then liberates hirself from the long cycle of incarnations — even then the mountain seems to stretch out into infinitude; yet the *Master* is now a very good climber indeed.

The word *Master* is used figuratively here, and indicates that a human being has in effect mastered hir lower nature, after having moved hir consciousness into the Spirit. Such people do not usually call themselves *Masters*, or *Mistresses* for that matter.

There is Higher Self within Higher Self; the infinite vanishing point ever vanishes into even Greater Planes of Existence and Life... i.e., there is no one level of Higher Self; the Higher Self is infinite; super-existent; and metanimated (not a word which you will find readily in today's dictionaries!).

This in fact presses a point: we do not really have any adequate words to describe what the Higher Self *is*, and what Hir Level of Consciousness is like. We have to make analogies to bring out some of the smaller aspects of Hir Truth. We try and describe Hir Being-ness with intellect, when S/he is beyond the intellect... which is probably why so many people end up resorting to emotional religions whenever they try and approach the Infinite Self, for whatever apparent reason; the lower intellect simply cannot absorb the full Reality of the God-dess/the Higher Life Principle; whereas emotions can at least react to quasi-spiritual superlatives, if poorly and inadequately.

The Higher Mind, or abstract intellect, however, once *Spiritualised* at a conscious level, can start to make some sense of the Cosmic Scheme. This leads certain Adepts to make *maps* — such as the information given out in the Mystery Schools, by genuine shamans, and in *ABC* form in certain books. Nevertheless, these *maps* are always and at best somewhat incomplete or else partial, if not a little *coloured*, and they cannot contain all the reference points which can be *known*. A traveller in the Beyond may choose to highlight what s/he has *seen*; yet what s/he has *seen* is only a very small part of the whole.

Undoubtedly, the clearest *map* which we can get hold of at present is based on the findings of the ancient Tibetans — they spent thousands of years exploring the Heavens, and as a result their information is of great interest to us now (the Spiral Publications books are largely based on Tibetan information, yet laced with *new* insights from *extra-terrestrial* sources). Many of the best methods of accessing the Beyond are shamanic in nature.

Meditate on all this — what does it mean to you?

12 — MEGATYPES

We all know what archetypes are (or do we?!). *Arch* — from the Greek *archein, to rule*; and *archi, chief* — indicates a life-principle. Therefore an archetype is an expression of a principle at a symbolic-to-actual level.

The implication is that archetypes form something of a conceptual root-essence, from which all other things are derived — i.e., that all *types* are related to a higher *archetype(s)* (this, incidentally, is what is meant by *animism* — the perception that all forms of organic (and inorganic) life have their origin in the Soul, and by implication, in the Spirit).

This is the basis for modern psychology — imperfect as the science of psychology may be, admittedly. The relevance of archetypes only really comes to life when we start talking about metaphysics, however; and especially about magick, and about the Higher Devas.

A megatype, by definition, is a *meta-archetype* — a *root of roots,* if you like. The Higher Self, if you will, is a megatype.

Nevertheless, the Higher Self we are alluding to is only the *smallest* of the megatypes; there are Megatypes beyond that, and these form part of the Cosmic Meta-structure; the Greater Cosmic Network — as *Beings-of-Principle*.

In other words, the Higher Self has its own Higher Self (much as a personality self has hir Higher Self — see how inadequate our language really is?! Where are the words to describe these different degrees of *Higher Self?!*).

The Tibetans identified a Being which they referred to as *Everness* (if one translates their word for *It*, that is). This Being *resides* on the 7th Cosmic Plane, i.e., on the 49th Plane of Existence — and for a moment you will be excused if the notion of 49 Planes rocks your incredulity! That Being in turn has Hir Higher Self (see THE COSMIC GOD-DESS; the seventh transmission in, and Section 20 of INITIATION, TRANSMUTATION & IMMORTALITY, in THE PSYCHIC EXPLORER).

Not that the highest Adepts on Earth have any real idea of

what *Everness* represents in terms of consciousness; so what can be made of, let us call Hir, "Meta-Everness"?

Meditate on that (there is no point telling you how to meditate; if you haven't learnt how to do that by now you have not been applying the information to be found in this book!).

The Cosmos is greater than we can possibly conceive of.

13 — COSMIC JOKES, AND COSMIC QUESTIONS

"If I exist, and simultaneously do not exist, what am I?" — answer: an impossible possibility! (and actuality).

"If I tell you that you are a mirage of a paradox, would you feel the same about yourself?"

"If I say that we are, collectively, the recipients of the Cosmic Avatar's descending energies, and that this energy is a ripple on the meta-surface of the Cosmic Ocean, how many ripples will it take before that energy reaches you?"

"If I say that positive response is directly akin to arising energies going back to their Source, and that the distance between you and the Source is infinite, how long will it takes you to reach that Source?" (There is only one viable answer, and it is the key to all Cosmic travel).

"Whenever there are two or more Adepts who agree perfectly about the Higher Self in every possible detail — it is because they have gone beyond detail."

"To be full is to be empty; how much emptiness constitutes ultimate fullness?"

"The Door to Infinity is an infinitely small Point; can you pass through It?"

14 — META-PROGRAMMING FACTORS

The universe that we experience daily is a projection of the mind; the Universe that an Adept experiences is a projection of the Spirit; the Super-Universe that a Cosmic Being experiences is a projection of the Cosmic One. The Meta-Infinite that a Meta-Cosmic Being experiences is ...

... No one within the Seven Cosmic Planes (i.e., 49 Planes) knows that.

Within ourselves, somewhere deep within, there are meta-programs — inner points of reference, if you like. These, of course, are not known to our ordinary minds yet they can be accessed in meditation, given enough power to do so.

Shamanism, or better yet direct *insight,* reveals that we are luminous beings, and that we are sphere-shaped. Within that sphere there are many different points where consciousness can be *moved to.* Each point, when used as a focus for one's consciousness, reveals a particular kind of perception, and a certain kind of power.

By learning to *shift* one's consciousness within the area of the sphere which deals with various aspects of the world, one can *see* that world in different ways, and then deal with things in different ways. *Moving* one's consciousness beyond that area into other areas can reveal aspect of the greater Universe around us, and within us.

Meditation ultimately is about learning to *shift*, and then *move* one's consciousness from one area to the next — thus one *sees* different aspects of Life, one draws on inner energies one never knew were there to be tapped, and eventually one learns how to master one's control over *shifting* and *moving* one's consciousness in this way, at will.

By *shifting* one's consciousness, even imperceptibly, within a given area of the sphere that one is, one can become identified with different principles — and thus one can greatly extend the repertoire of one's abilities. This is the art of the shaman/ka, or sorcer/ess (or *sourcer/ess*).

By *moving* one's consciousness out of that area altogether, into other areas, one becomes identified with principles, or meta-programs, which are no longer of the human kind — one's perceptions of the Life which surrounds us then become so radically different that if one stays focused in a *far-point* for too long one then *moves out* of the human evolutionary stream altogether... into what will depend on which *far-point* one's consciousness was focused on.

Shamankas (women shamans) are usually better at *shifting* and *moving* their consciousness or attention than are male shamans — because they are less likely to try and be logical about what it is that is happening. Logic, or *reason*, is one particular point within the sphere, and it interferes with, or negates, the perceptions one can have from the vantage of other points.

If one is not prepared for these *shifts,* and particularly for complete *movements* of one's attention, it is easy to become very distressed — because one *connects* one's consciousness with powers which one is not at all used to.

Against that, the potential for self-transformation is dramatic — we are beings of energy; by *aligning* one's consciousness with a given point within the sphere one can *become the principle* embodied within that point; that principle itself if encoded energy; therefore one becomes that encoded energy.

This will have far-reaching consequences which one then has to learn to deal with — with power, with *intent*, and with balance. Nothing that can be written can divulge what it is that one will have to learn, however; one can only learn by *going there*.

15 — *THE SOURCE OF THE DNA BIO-COMPONENT*

Physically we are not genetic accidents, once we go back to the consideration of our little human selves. The essential DNA helix pattern within our chromosomes is a reflection of cosmic processes; it is then modified by energy-events, including dense biological events.

In this it does not differ too significantly from the systemic helix where we find the planets of a Solar System orbiting a sunstar in a spiral motion.

Or in the expression of Kundalini/Shakti energy.

Or in the three-to-four dimensional expression of the chakras.

Or in the spiral process of a galaxy.

Or in the impregnated ovum whirling counter-clockwise in a

fallopian tube before it descends into the womb.

Or in the way that bath water vortexes down into the exit pipe.

Spirals are the key to all of Life's *transferral* activities.

Even an incarnating human being is drawn down into physical existence by a widdershins current or vortex (... and what is the impregnated ovum doing?).

Likewise a Master Adept departs from physical existence on a deosil (clockwise) upsurging current of energy; while a Master Adept who remains in incarnation balances that current with a perfectly synchronised descending deosil current, which is widdershins to the deosil upsurge of primal Shakti. And uses hir Will to remain rooted on the physical plane.

... Food for meditation.

INTERLUDE 3

It is one thing to perceive something of the heights accessible to one's internal consciousness; it is another to put this into a useful context with regard to one's everyday life.

To the average person the Mysteries of the Inner Life do not hold much, if any reality; s/he cannot see them, and is even less well equipped to understand them even at a theoretical level — assuming that s/he might read about them somewhere, which in itself is relatively unlikely.

To the Adept — if we define such a human being as one who has gone some way towards liberating hirself from the need to incarnate, and everything which that entails — the juxtaposition of inner vision and outer world living poses something of a problem, at least initially — how does one reconcile the need for carrying on with all one's outer world affairs, when the inner worlds are beckoning for more and more attention? And yet it is necessary to put one's personal life into a new and better order, thereby allowing for more flexibility; and as a result a choice of paths becomes apparent — several of which paths may seem attractive, because each one offers something of an opening into the unknown — nevertheless each one of which is based on the needs of one's present.

There are many, many paths, and yet when seen from a more essential point of view there are only three main Paths — out of which all the others emerge.

CHAPTER 4 — THE CHOICE OF PATHS

16 — THE PATH OF SERENITY

You are meditating on top of a hill; the Sun is setting in the West. You are completely open to the forces of Nature; you feel completely natural; nothing disturbs you — you feel in perfect equilibrium.

You feel calm, poised, strong, and yet gentle as well; and very loving towards Life.

You feel intoxicated by the beauty of what you see — the inner streams of subtle energies superimposed on the glory of the outside world of the setting Sun... At that moment you feel in conscious contact with thousands, maybe even millions of years of evolution. You feel yourself to be an intrinsic part of the Life which surrounds you, and especially with that which is active or resident within you. You feel at peace; and you feel something undescribable — it is like a re-union; a going-back to the Spirit. Real Life; real living.

You k*now* that this is a promise which has come down through the ages — the promise of permanent liberation.

You are not quite *there* yet, nevertheless you *know* that it will not be too long now before that promise unfolds further and becomes complete. There is no need to rush; it is almost like a natural, organic process — it has its momentum, and it will happen.

At length you realise that one *grows* back into the Spirit; it occurs degree by degree, with a few peaks from time to time to accelerate this process, or accentuate it. Bit by bit the *picture* forms, and that picture is transparent; one *sees* it without seeing it.

You are meditating on a beach; it is early morning. The Sun has just risen lazily over the sea, casting gentle beams of light on an unsuspecting day.

Streams of energy-impressions are reaching the forefront of your consciousness — subtle in their contents, and yet powerful in their informative value. You feel inspired; the morning of the day is like the morning of a new life on another Level of Existence.

Water from the shore is trickling out to the sea as the tide moves out; you watch a bubble on its surface, moving towards the vast ocean in front of you ... and you *know* that Nature is helping you to *see* and appreciate what you are doing yourself — you are moving, inexorably, towards the vastness of Infinity... and soon you will be merging into that deeper, higher world... in full consciousness; fully alert. Fully aware. Ready, without really knowing yet what you are ready for.

It feels the most natural thing that could be — hidden from the ordinary eye, and yet so simple when *seen*.

You feel united with Life, and It is a friend; It *speaks* to you softly, with power.

You are in a wood. The trees seem sensuous; they are there, and also *not there*. You rest your back on one of them for a while, and watch the sky through the branches. You are surrounded by everything and nothing; you see the outer world... and yet for all intents and purposes it is only an image. You turn around, and embrace the tree, talking to it gently without words — acknowledging that your life and its life are but One Life.

You put your forehead on its bark to be more at-one with it. At that moment it becomes an all important friend — different from you, and yet also the same.

A while later you kiss it — like a lover, very genuinely, very lovingly, very gently. A caress of lips on its existence. You thank it for being there.

You are in a ravine. A stream of torrential white water gushes between the rocks; you sit by the water, meditating on the power of Nature's expression... The power of moving water.

You feel filled with energy; cleansed by the power...

The sunlight catches on the surface of the cliffs, speckled with the colours of wild flowers...

You are meditating on the clouds. They move like landscapes across the sky: high mountains, hilly crests, deep notches into unknown sky-borne valleys... Like the inner worlds they cannot be walked upon with a dense physical body; and yet how beautiful it would be to walk on them regardless!

You are walking on the site of an ancient place, where people once lived, surrounded by the same, and yet a different world. You can sense something of their perspective, the way they lived their lives — mothers preparing food and working basketry; children playing in the water of the lake; men fishing... Their moments of magick; their moments of difficulty... Perhaps you were there back then, looking at that hill yonder; at that field... What has really changed? A lot, and yet very little.

A bird flies by... Then a second.

... Like thoughts flying away from one age into another.

You are meditating in a woodland clearing. The Sun is warming your body as a faint breeze passes by; butterflies are dancing all around you. You are listening to a bird singing, very purely... delightful in its nuances; and its message is full of heart.

A superior bird, in its moment of revelation.

You are becoming the world around you — each facet of what you see and feel is a facet of your unfolding life.

You are meditating on the inner worlds, and supported by the interlaced vision of Nature and Super-Nature you feel utterly serene.

Your whole life becomes an extension of that serenity... even those practical activities with which you must deal are subject to its influence.

17 — THE PATH OF CREATIVITY

Inspirited by your perceptions, a path of creative expression may well suit you best. It feels entirely natural to you to be creative; to express your perceptions in some manner or other.

This may be prompted by a spontaneous feeling of wanting to communicate your findings to others, sharing with them something of what you have *seen;* and maybe you just feel you want to create because it is beautiful to do so.

Creativity can be objective — like making something; and it can also be subjective: for example, the way that you meditate can be creative: thought-forms drawn into association, given power, and released on the ethers to inspire others, to help things happen, to manifest a new living ambience.

Much of what never comes to fruition in life derives its failure from a lack of internal ability to cohere those forces which can be given expression; a project fails, because the mind or minds behind it are unable to support their vision, step by step, until it takes on outward reality; and then to be flexible enough so that the creation does not become stagnant or overly crystallised.

Creativity is a constant process of visualising that which can be, and making it happen, bit by bit — paying attention to each detail as one goes along; taking advantage of one's natural or acquired talents; and being as practical as one may be visionary.

The balance between practicality and one's creative vision is paramount; the one without the other is unproductive. It is indeed a bane to be highly practical, yet to have no vision; and it is equally unhelpful to be inspired, yet unable to be in the least bit practical.

If this applies at a general level, it applies even more so in the case of an initiate, for an initiate has even less of an excuse not to be more coherent in hir expression. After all, attaining a state of liberation is in itself a creative work — because everything that one does should add to one's success in this; each step should have meaning, if not significance.

It then becomes a question of which *projects* to apply oneself to — projects that will reflect one's internal efforts, and in some way objectify them.

This is discussed at length in THE POWER OF CREATIVE VISUALISATION, a sister book to this one.

18 — THE PATH OF POWER

Ego power is one thing — it is usually ugly in its expression, glorifying as it does the individual at the expense of others. In a materialistic society this is so much in evidence that it scarcely requires further comment.

At the other end of things one finds allegedly spiritual exhortations to be totally selfless; to dedicate oneself to the good of the all at the expense of one's individuality.

Both of these extremes are equally redundant.

What really matters is to find and encourage balance in one's life; to promote the good of the all, as well as one's own personal, individual needs.

The way of power is essential to any Spiritual growth, because even if there are those who will dwell more on the side of power than, say, on the side of *love*, or on the side of mind, power in itself is what animates all expression.

Power is not *wrong;* it does not necessarily corrupt, as the catch-phrase goes. An expression of creativity is an act of power; an expression of love, likewise, has its own power.

All life is power — because all manifested life is energy in expression.

Power only corrupts those who hog power entirely to themselves in a totally selfish way, instead of sharing it with others in some desirable manner, without depleting themselves.

To illustrate this at a mundane level: if we consider momentarily the different political ideologies presently dominant within this world, we may — if we look deeply enough — see different prototype fractions of what may become the way of politics in the future.

At the present time there is no such thing as a democracy, any more than there is any genuine expression of communism. Democracy means that the power-to-rule is shared by consensus — yet people are herded into making predefined choices which do not truly allow a sharing of that power; in the communist system, the principle is that everything is shared, and yet laws are made so rigid that — as in political democracies — an elite (often of old men) rules over the people.

Nevertheless, the principle of individual freedom is right, as is the principle of collective sharing. What is wrong is that an elite should dictate to the many, and that the many should allow this to occur.

Within the sphere of influence that each system represents — however imperfect these systems may be — there are prototypes of social life which, when blended, rather than opposed, could lead to a type of socio-politics which would maximise everything which is desirable, and quell everything which is not.

But how does one define what is desirable? And would everyone agree?

Much the same questions must be asked of oneself when one is dealing with one's own individual processes: how should one express the power which runs through oneself, especially at an initiatic level?

The answer in the end is simple: if it promotes a balanced, flowing and creative way of living, then it should be promoted; if it does not, then it should be relinquished or left alone.

Our world has become, in some ways, so individualistic that it lacks unitive cohesion; and this is precisely why meditation is so useful — because it links us with all Life; it brings us into union with the All.

An act of true power is to cause an effect which is viable, creative and desirable. Once one acknowledges that all life is One Life, then one cannot go about subjugating others to one's personal will. The Universal Spiritual Will (Atma) is the only Way of Power.

Flowing with Life is the Only Way.

Allowing the Spirit to *move* through oneself is the *Way of Power* — that is to *do* the Will of the Spirit; to *act* as the Spirit *moves one to act*.

Only then can one tread the Path of Power.

INTERLUDE 4

There are those who will say of this book that it does not document meditation as practised in the East; the answer to this is two-fold:

(1) This is quite correct, it does not (despite the information of Tibetan origin)... If you are thinking of Yoga-type meditations which require a special training period before they can be applied fully, then it is best to learn that kind of meditation in the East, or from an Eastern teacher — for the most part it is of little use in the West anyway; we simply do not live an Eastern way of life.

(2) People still have many misconceptions about meditation, and tend to make differentiations between meditation, contemplation, visualisation, attunement and alignment. However, all five of these are forms of meditation.

In the end it is what you get out of meditation — and how you feel inclined to explore your inner and outer potential — which is important.

The ways of meditating are endless. Your imagination and sensitivity, and the amount of power that you bring into your meditations, are your only limits.

The Chapter which follows deals with several meditations which can be practised in different places. It begins with Nature-oriented meditations, then graduates towards more abstract meditations, and ends up with Cosmic alignments.

What is the true purpose of meditation?

(1) Learning to relax body, emotions and mind.

(2) Centring one's attention and focus of consciousness.

(3) Reaching out (or reaching in) for Life.

(4) Cultivating the ability to tune in to Life.

(5) Identifying with a situation for the sake of experience.

(6) Identifying oneself with one's Higher Self, and with Higher Life Principles.

(7) Making conscious contact with Cosmic Sources through alignment.

What are the results of doing this?

(1) Becoming more sensitive psychically and Spiritually.

(2) Learning to alter one's consciousness at will.

(3) Increasing the vibratory rate of one's energy-fields.

(4) Improving the quality of one's life and expression.

(5) Learning to Live (resulting in transcendence).

CHAPTER 5 — POWER MEDITATIONS

19 — NATURE MEDITATIONS

Seek an affinitive location high up in the hills — on a reasonably clear day.

Create a circle on the ground (about 6 feet in diameter) around the spot you have chosen for your meditation — use twelve small stones, which you feel good about; walking on the outside of your intended circle, place one stone in the East, and then moving clockwise, one in the South, then one in the West, and one in the North.

Now the mid-points: one in the South East, one in the South West, one in the North West, and one in the North East.

Walk around (still clockwise) to the South; calm your thoughts for a moment; then knock gently on the stone in the South three times with your index knuckle and ask the Directional Powers for permission to enter the Circle you have just made. If you feel that permission has been granted, then enter the Circle through the South.

Now place one stone below the North point, then one in the South; then one in the East, and one in the West; you now have two delineated Circles — one made up of eight stones, and one made up of four stones.

Enter the inner Circle delineated by the four stones..

Face the East, and invoke the Power of the East — you can talk aloud, or else you can talk silently within yourself. "Power of the East, come to me. Bring me inspiration and new energies."

Now face the South. "Power of the South, come to me. Lend me power and open the Door of Fire."

Now on to the West. "Power of the West, come to me. Initiate me to the Mysteries of Nature and Super-Nature."

And finally the North. "Power of the North, come to me. Give me strength and balance."

Then sit down in the inner Circle, facing the East. Breathe deeply and meditate on the Power of the East — try and feel it, and what it represents. After a while face the South, and do likewise. Then the West; and then the North.

Finally, face the direction to which you feel most drawn within yourself — including one of the mid-points, if pertinent — i.e., if you feel that is what you should do; or if you feel this is what you are being guided to do by the Directional Powers; or by your Higher Self, or by the Spirit (all three are the same thing really).

Acquaint yourself thoroughly with the Directional Force which you are facing — knowing that all the others are there also, assisting you; yet these are in the background only.

Go deep into your meditation. Breathe very deeply; there are no thoughts in your mind; your eyes are closed.

Then allow impressions or visions to come to you — you are there to learn and to attune yourself... If you feel a need to do so, ask a question of personal importance, and wait for the answer to form in your mind's eye.

If the answer does not come it is because you are not yet ready for it. If it does come, then focus your whole attention on it — without forcing anything; just let it resolve itself into clarity for you.

It is often best to ask only one question, and to use your meditation to get the one answer. Sometimes, however, you may be presented with a number of choices — in which case look at each choice in turn; and then focus on the one which draws you most.

If you feel that it is right to do so, you can ask other questions — facing the Directional Power which you feel can give you the answers you require.

If your questions are tinged with ego, then the answers may be complete nonsense, or else highly convoluted, or else will mock you to the point of absolute ridicule; or you may get no answer at all; or, fifthly, and more *dangerously,* you may experience one or several energy warnings (which usually come in the form of subjective bolts of lightning).

If your questions are put to the Directional Force in all humility, with respect, then you will get clear and worthwhile answers.

An option is to keep your eyes open — focusing these on the horizon — and to wait for a *sign*, or omen. The *sign* may come to you through the medium of any natural event which may occur around you — for instance, the flight of a bird; a cloud of a particular shape; a sudden breeze; etc. Then it is up to you to *see* it for what it is, and to interpret it correctly.

At the close of your meditation give heartful thanks to each of the Directional Powers — facing these in turn as before; dismantle the inner Circle (counter-clockwise this time); then walk out of the outer Circle through the South, and dismantle the outer Circle (also widdershins).

Unless the Circle is intended to be pe*rmanent* — i.e., inaccessible to others — always dismantle it, and leave no physical trace of your *activity* there.

Banish the accumulated energies by waving your right hand (palm facing downwards) over the spot — back and forth repeatedly, while imagining that the energies are being dispersed evenly in all directions, until none are left. Then thank the area for allowing you to do your meditation there.

If it is a *permanent* site, face the North, then seal (i.e., protect) the energies there by describing (with your right hand), first a circle, then a cross within the circle, and finally a pentagram (starting with the topmost apex, then down to the lower right, over to the upper left, across to the upper right, down to lower left, and back to the apex). Projecting the colour blue is useful in this instance (or white; or violet if you practise magick there).

As you become more acquainted with the practice of using a Circle of this kind, you will find, degree by degree, that you will be taught many deep things about Nature and the natural world — including about Super-Nature; and also about yourself. Nebulous results will give way to very clear answers, and then increasingly you will be shown various subtleties with regard to Devas, etc.

As a *newcomer* or *neophyte* to the Circle, you should always approach and enter it through the South; and initially you should also leave it through the South. Later, when you are stronger and feel more able you can choose to enter it through any *Directional Gate* you wish, and also depart from it through any other Gate — always with sensitivity and respect, however.

This method is derived from the American Indian Medicine Wheels, and should be seen as an adapted variation of these.

You can create a Circle in other places as well; but avoid the sides of rivers and streams, and water holes, and to a lesser extent lakes and seas — unless you feel you know what you are doing.

You can also create the Circle symbolically without using any stones, although it is best to acquaint yourself with the Circle by using stones to begin with.

If you want *to do it* the American Indian way, then find a good teacher who knows the Power and Way of the Medicine Wheels.

20 — ABSTRACT MEDITATIONS

To be practised anywhere that is quiet. Enter into your meditation, and allow all your thoughts to dissipate, until none are left — your mind is now still; your emotions are in abeyance.

Then picture in your mind a huge, very tall dark room. You are in the dark. Then see a small aperture in the upper part of one of the walls, or ceiling — white light is coming in through that gap. It strikes a four-sided pyramid, with its apex pointing upwards; the pyramid is made of clear *thought-form* crystal.

The white light is diffracted into the seven colours of the rainbow. Choose one of the colours, and then project your consciousness along that ray, into the crystal pyramid; then, as white light, project at high speed up towards the aperture where the light is coming through.

Enter the Higher Worlds, and *see* what you will.

Same as before; this time see the Seven Esoteric Rays: Violet for Rhythmic or Ceremonial Magick; Rose-Red or Pink for Ideas; Indigo-Blue for Analytical Focus; Golden-Yellow for Artistic Creativity and Harmony; Green for Mind and Communication; Light-Blue for Serenity, Revelation and Love-Wisdom; and Red for Power, Will and Purpose. Project your consciousness along one of these Rays, and as you exit the pyramid and reach up into the Higher Worlds, keep your focus on that Ray.

Another abstract meditation: visualise yourself in a clear, yet slightly blue-tinted sphere. Now breathe deeply, and as you do so, breathe in more and more blue light through the top of the sphere — until the sphere is radiating with that blue light — it is an electric colour (white light can be used as an alternative).

The sphere is now your *spaceship*, so to speak; you can go anywhere you like with it, and you will be perfectly protected by it — and you will be able to see anything you like through it.

You can go to various locations on and off the Earth; or you can go into other dimensions: the Astral Plane (the dimension of living dreams); the Mental Plane (where thought-forms take on definition and existence); the Buddhic or Harmonic Plane (filled with harmonious, unitive energies — where you will feel at-One with all of Life, including everything that you *see*; where intuitions will guide you, inspire you and reveal things to your consciousness; where you will feel united with your soul; with the world's Soul; where you will feel *Great Love*; where you will meet your Solar Deva); the Atm(a)ic Plane (the Level of Will and Purpose — powerful energies... and *intent*); the Monadic Plane (where you will encounter your Cosmic or Higher Self); the Systemic Plane, or Plane of Adi (where your consciousness will merge with that of the Sun, and the Solar System as a Being).

Of course you will only really access these Higher Planes if you are capable of doing so — yet you can always try anyway. It requires power, perfect attention, and absolute *stillness* within.

You should note that the sphere has an electro-magnetic axis, running from top to bottom. This is coincident with your spine.

The more you can activate your Kundalini or Shakti energy, the more you will have the power to take the sphere, and therefore yourself, to where you want to go — in consciousness.

If at any point you feel in dis-equilibrium — out-of-balance — then *align* yourself and the sphere with the star Polaris (the Northern Star). It might be worth your while acquainting yourself with that star on clear nights first. This star acts as a magnetic pointer for the whole planet at this time.

A third abstract meditation: above you you see a point of light. The point expands to reveal a vortex of energy, spiraling clockwise, and it begins to draw you upwards. To begin with, resist its attractive power, and allow this force to build up. Finally, when you can resist it no longer, when the effort to remain *earthed* is overcome by the upward current, then let go completely without any reservations or fear, and allow yourself to be drawn up into the Unknown (this is a very powerful meditation, or consciousness projection technique; it should only be used when you are already well acquainted with other types of meditation).

A fourth abstract meditation, similar in some respects to the one immediately above: imagine yourself — as vividly as you can — to be on the outside of a large circular platform. This platform is divided into three concentric rings; the outer ring is green; the middle ring is light-blue; and the inner ring is red.

From the periphery of the outer ring, a lattice of white light energy is drawn upwards into a Power Cone. At the top of the Power Cone there is an infinitely small Point — which is in fact a Star-Gate. The lattice of energy is whirling counter-clockwise from the base of the platform up to that Gate (therefore clockwise in relation to seeing that Point from below). Enter the platform, and very slowly walk your way in perfect consciousness, still visualising everything as vividly as you can, towards the centre of the platform. *Feel* what it is like to be in the green ring, and charge up with its energy; then pass through the threshold into the light-blue ring — *feel* the light-blue ring, and charge up with that energy; then go through the threshold into the red inner circle; *feel* what that one is like, and again, charge up with the energy there. Go to the very centre of the platform, then allow yourself to be projected at high speed through the apex of the Power Cone, therefore through the Star-Gate... again into the Unknown... or to any place and/or any Plane you wish to go to (you will have to keep that place in mind throughout your meditation, or else you should think of it at the last possible moment before your projection takes place; using appropriate symbols to access such places is useful - for instance, the glyph for Venus if you want to reach that planet).

A fifth abstract meditation: meditate on the idea of becoming gradually very, very small... until you have become a tiny point of consciousness. Then expand that point of consciousness until it becomes infinitely big, thereby encompassing all of Infinity (this is not as easy as it sounds).

21 — COSMIC ALIGNMENTS

An ali*gnment* is, in theory, the shortest link of energy between two or more places, or beings (or consciousness streams). Within the context of the Cosmic Network there are many such *alignments* already in situ — created by those beings (particularly certain types of Stellar Beings and Devas) who work with the energies of specific stars and planets.

Much of this information is never made public, although various hints are available in ESOTERIC ASTROLOGY by Alice A. Bailey.

For the purpose of this Section on *Cosmic Alignments*, avail yourself of a star map — a good one preferably; or a good star book will suffice (CONSTELLATIONS by Josef Klepesta and Antonin Rukl (Hamlyn) is an excellent little book for this purpose). Then meditate on those stars with which you feel a particular affinity.

Choose a star — the one you feel most drawn to — and imagine that there is a clear, direct bridge of energy between you and it; then in meditation project your consciousness along this bridge to that star.

Practise this until you succeed — it's not so easy.

In the mean time you can just meditate on the feelings you may have, including images, etc. Make notes of these after each meditation, and *visit* that star as frequently and as regularly as you can.

Then visit other stars in the same way.

Finally, go to the first star, then from there go to the second — using a bridge from the first star to the second; then likewise to the third; and so on...

Over a period of months expand on this network until you can visit at least 12 stars in one single meditation — in the right sequence; then go back the way you came until you reach the Earth again; alternatively reach back towards the Earth from the 12th star.

Once you have managed to do this — properly, and as vividly as possible — and then only, expand the network further, and include up to 49 stars.

The more you become sensitive to the qualities of the energy-emanations from different stars, the more you will start to to become intuitive as to their true nature as stellar beings. The more you *visit* certain affinitive stars in the right sequence, the more you will be able to store up within yourself something of their individual and collective evolutionary information and power.

However, there is no point doing any of this if you are not doing it for the right reasons... which is to bring back to Earth information-energies which will be genuinely useful here from an evolutionary point of view.

There are responsibilities involved as well. As you become *aligned* with different stellar beings, you will become as an *agent* for their own purposes — which collectively will be a subset of the overall Cosmic Purpose with regard to the Earth, the Sun, and the Solar System.

Therefore it is a two way process: (on behalf of the Earth) you will be availing yourself of what they have to offer; and they will be availing themselves of your *agency* with regard to *informing the Earth* — through you, as a channel.

To become an *agent* is not just a responsibility, however. The energies of stellar beings are enormously powerful, and therefore very demanding on one's relatively frail human make-up. The more you *align* yourself with these beings, the more they will *come through*, resulting in surcharges of energy which you will have to deal with in a highly balanced way.

You will need to learn how to *hold off* those energies when the build-up becomes too great; to *filter* those energies in a discriminating and intuitive fashion whenever necessary; and to harmonise your own energy-field at all times especially at peak moments when the process may become almost overwhelming.

Also the ambient elemental energies around you may react strongly to the inflow of extra-systemic energies, creating difficulties for you, and possibly difficulties for others (reading STARCRAFT, which is a part of this series of manuals, is highly recommended).

Against that, these beings often approach the Earth as projected consciousness, and they do so very slowly, in relative terms. They are very aware of the potential dangers of *coming in* too soon or too quickly.

Above all else your responsibility is towards the Earth as a Spiritual Being. You will need to learn to ask the Earth what *S/he* needs before *bringing in* energies from elsewhere — and what is more, you will need to learn to do this as instantaneously as possible... which requires a lot of intuitive sensitivity.

To put this in a different way, you are (or would be) first and foremost an evolutionary *agent* of behalf of the Earth (and by implication, on behalf of the Sun and the whole Solar System). The Earth is continually informed and influenced by extra-systemic sources, nevertheless there is an element of emphasis or discrimination at work — and this through all those beings (initiates and devas, insofar as we need be concerned here) who act as intelligent, intuitive and purposeful *agents* or channels on behalf of the whole planet. At any one time — including at peak moments — there must be a striving for balance; if the overall equilibrium was to become too disturbed this could lead to undesirable, if not somewhat disastrous results.

It is not your prerogative to upset the planetary balance; nor should you feel that you are shouldering any particular burden on your own — nor should you think that you have the power to do so. Whenever an initiate is involved in agency work or channelling of this kind, there are other High Adepts (unseen) who are carefully monitoring what is going on, and these will always lend assistance to any one individual caught up in the process (unless the individual is acting negatively, and deliberately so — in which case they will not lend any assistance at all, and will be more concerned with neutralising any possible havoc which wrong doing might precipitate; wrong doing in this context leads to self-destruction).

Finally, redefining meditation once more: meditation is the method whereby one becomes acquainted with the Cosmic domain as an *agent* on behalf of Cosmic Purpose/the Cosmic Oneness.

With Love and Wisdom; and by channelling the Power of the Spirit.

INTERLUDE 5

We are fast advancing into a New Age whose parameters of growth are still largely unknown to us. Many choices confronts us, and the choices we actually make will determine much of what will happen in the next century, and beyond.

Taking into account that it is the 7th Ray of Rhythmic Magick which will predominantly influence this period of our planetary unfoldment — a Ray-influence which culminates in synthesis, which is the key to its process — we will see changes such as we have never seen or experienced before.

For a moment let us try and understand what synthesis *actually means in this context.*

At this time humanity has put together a large body of relative knowledge, and this is particularly noticeable from a scientific point of view, although we must also widen our appreciation of what constitutes knowledge.

Facts are knowledge, nevertheless in some respects facts are somewhat arbitrary or relative, and one type of fact — pertaining to a particular area of knowledge does not necessarily mean that other types of facts pertaining to that same area are not true, even if initially different sets of facts may not seem compatible. One definite finding does not rule out the validity of other findings; one theory, however aesthetic it may be, does not necessarily make all other theories redundant or false, particularly when seen from different points of view.

As theories evolve out of the situations which give rise to their expression we sometimes discard perceptions which still have power. Accumulating these perceptions, and constantly re-evaluating their usefulness in the light of new perceptions, we derive new, more holistic points of view.

We must also resist the temptation to see life only in terms of nuts and bolts. *Much by way of useful knowledge can be gained from more subjective processes, including various types of clairvoyance, particularly during moments of peak experience. We live in a physical universe, yet we also live in a psychic and Spiritual universe, and perceptions derived from moments of heightened consciousness can lead us towards new areas of investigation and realisation.*

Seen from this angle, and considering that world-wide there are people who are exploring life in as yet unconventional ways — inasmuch as their findings are not always acknowledged by those who think of themselves as scientific, for instance (although to be scientific includes the notion that information should be proven wrong before it is rejected, rather than proven right before it is accepted) — we have the basis for a new understanding of life. And we need this new understanding, for without it our accepted truths will not give us the bridgeway we require before we embark fully into this New Age.

CHAPTER 6 — THE BRIDGEWAY

22 — THE EXTRA-TERRESTRIAL FACTOR

We live in an interactive universe, and the sooner we acknowledge this fully, the sooner we can come to terms with the presence of extra-terrestrial intelligences around us (and even amongst us).

As a planetary civilisation we output energy, and that energy is information-energy to those who might care to tune into it. Viewing causes rather than effects, a higher intelligence would first perceive the roots of any given unfoldment, and then look at the consequences of its expression (rather than the other way around).

To view life as the interaction of positive and negative energies, and to classify positive as *good* and negative as *evil*, is a dualistic misconception. All positive and negative aspects of expression are relative, and therefore not in the least bit *fixed*.

It is this dualistic misconception which has been the cause of much suffering that we have witnessed over the past two thousand years and more. Conceptual opposites have given rise to polarised attitudes and actions which have generated unavoidable frictions, followed by conflicts. We can see this at work politically as the dualism between *capitalist* and *communist* idealism, which has taken us to the edge of a possible planetary nuclear holocaust.

One wo/man's *God* is another wo/man's *Devil* — and each side views itself as right, and the other as wrong.

The fact is neither side is right or wrong, or alternatively each side is both right and wrong.

An intelligent observer can appreciate these relativities, and then look for the creative possibilities inherent to the apparent or actual conflicts of interests. The *synthetic* (and therefore creative) approach is to look for all those denominators which can be usefully merged rather than destroyed by misplaced antagonism.

This gives way to a new type of balance — not one held in situ by a balance of power based on the threat of mutual annihilation, but one which strives to combine the best of both systems — each system being something of an experiment in structural living and expression, each producing useful results, as well as results which are not so useful or acceptable.

This fusion creates a new, superior system — a natural extension of the experiments so far undertaken and unfolded.

Extending this notion further, we can begin to perceive a greater input from other *systems*. As a planetary civilisation we represent a particular type of evolution. When we juxtapose this with all the ambient, extra-terrestrial evolutions around us we are faced with the need for an even greater balance and resolution of forces.

Taking up the information to be found in section 21 — Cosmic Alignments — we can start to acknowledge that there are evolutions around us which do influence us, and which can influence us further if we consciously open ourselves to their perspectives. In turn we have an influence on them, because everything that we do or express affects them, directly or indirectly.

By accepting this extended perspective of the situation we can look for those pointers which could prove useful in this respect — i.e., which would help us to achieve a greater balance.

Making the assumption that different civilisations in different places, and in this case on different planets, evolve from an original state of immaturity into a state of ever-increasing maturity, much of which maturity consists of intelligent and intuitive responses to new perspectives, we can look for ways of communicating intelligently, intuitively, and therefore fruitfully with other evolutions. Our initial difficulty is in recognising the content and intent of a given communication when it reaches us in a form which we cannot comprehend.

We have choices in our approach to resolving this problem. We can either elect to learn their languages or communication modes, and/or they can elect to learn ours. Or we can evolve a new, even if only temporary *language*, which will permit both sides to communicate with each other during the initial stages of contact.

The latter approach is often the only one which will bring about a more immediate recognition that communication is actually taking place — each side being prepared to evolve a common method of communicating which will suit each side's purposes well.

The art or act of *channelling* is in itself a communication mode, since it permits a channel to accept the throughput of information as impulses of meaning, which can then be translated into a known form of general communication for the benefit of others. Channelling in this sense is a kind of universal telepathy.

The information itself can be in the form of direct transmissions (high-powered telepathic communications); staggered transmissions (chains of inputs-outputs from a higher source through a network of receivers-communicators acting from different levels, reducing the frequency of the energy at each stage, and finally received by the channel(s); or casual, and usually subtle transmissions (the channel is more or less well acquainted with the communication source(s)).

We then have the possibility of presenting the information imparted in various subset modes.

First of all the impulses may be viewed as encoded transmissions of light. The person acting as a channel deciphers those light-codes (consciously to subconsciously), and translates these into an overall *sense* of meaning, then into units of meaning, and finally into a language which we use. This process is quasi-instantaneous in the case of a trained channel.

Then the transmissions can be presented literally as *messages*, or as information embedded in a medium of accepted communication (book text, film, artwork, etc.).

The accuracy of the reception will vary with the channel and hir level of aptitude in deciphering inputs; if s/he involves hir own thought-forms in the process then some *coloration* will take place.

To say that impulses are encoded transmissions of light is not enough, however. If the source is a relatively high one, acting from, say, the Monadic Plane, then that light is transferred to and *modulated* through a first receiver-communicator on the Atmic Plane; then through another on the Buddhic Plane, and so on until the *message* is received by the channel operating on the physical plane through a physical brain. If that channel turns out to be an Adept, then there is no specific need for intermediary receivers-communicators since an Adept can function consciously on all these Planes.

If the source is from a superior Cosmic Plane, then it is highly unlikely that the transmission will be received in its original content form. The transmission received will be a subset of a much more far-ranging transmission which is addressing itself to many evolutions on different Planes simultaneously, and quite possibly in different places as well, through a whole host of receivers-communicators-interpreters. The message is *diluted* and fragmented at each stage of the *descent* of that transmission; and the bit received will be the portion of the message which is designed to reach us selectively by inverse increments.

Seen from this perspective our relationship with what we may choose to call extra-terrestrial intelligences is intrinsic to the downflow of energy-communications from higher sources of influence and inspiration. A civilisation which views and experiences itself as a part of the Cosmic Network will willingly communicate information to a lesser civilisation in need of this information. By doing so it is opening the door for that lesser civilisation, and offering it the possibility of evolving into a state of consciousness whereby that communication and interaction will take place more directly on an ever-higher level.

Therefore if we are presently surrounded by extra-terrestrial civilisations which are ready to communicate with us it is because we are being *offered membership* into the Cosmic State, or Network.

In a situation such as the one we are beginning to experience at this time the first line of contact will be with civilisations which are only *slightly* more advanced than ours — they can relate better to our needs. Nevertheless, we might think of them as considerably more advanced because of the relativities involved.

The second line of contact will be with merged civilisations — i.e., with civilisations which have fused their essences and capabilities to the extent that they effectively form a *synthetic* civilisation based on complete mutuality and on a recognition of their intrinsic Oneness (many of the *messages* received and published by Spiral Publications have been from these types of sources).

The third line of contact will be with Cosmic Civilisations which have transcended the seven Planes in which we presently live and have our being.

All these lines of contact are already open, if only embryonically — something which may come as a surprise to many people.

These lines of contact will widen as more and more of us tune into the Network and derive information from this facility. At a key point in (our) time that contact will be symbolically opened to public consciousness, and an event of global proportions will take place; and this will represent an *official* overture.

This overture can only take place when the possibility of a nuclear holocaust has been finally and comprehensively neutralised — i.e., when humans will have overcome their propensity for dualism and conflict.

Therefore the timing for this overture is largely up to us.

23 — *INDIVIDUAL CHANNELLING*

Anyone who has any (even latent) psychic sensitivity, who is reasonably balanced within hirself, and who is prepared to embrace the Cosmic View can become a channel, or an *agent* on behalf of the Cosmic Network. Unlike formal situations which might require a specific form of application, the only requirement here is the unconditional willingness to *change* and to become ever more flexible and adaptive with regard to unusual pressures which may be brought about by the influx of new energies at a conscious level.

With this in mind the books issued by SPIRAL PUBLICATIONS (and many others) have been designed to accommodate enough information to make this possible.

24 — GROUP CHANNELLING

As we learn to work together for a common purpose — that of liberating the Earth's present civilisation from its relative isolation of consciousness with regard to the rest of Life — then we can communicate amongst ourselves, and with other civilisations, in order to bring about those necessary changes which will make further communication and intercourse possible.

... And in the process activate an ever-higher level of consciousness for ourselves, individually and collectively.

This can be viewed as group channelling.

As we learn to reciprocate intelligently, intuitively and purposefully with the universe around us, and within us, we will come to realise that there is such a State as Union. And that Unity-in-Diversity is the *Key* to the Cosmic Network.

As the communication lines reach more and more people, and are presented in such a manner that the information can be understood by different *consciousness groups*, then the essential *message* will become accessible to all.

All this, and much more, will revolutionise the way that we live — physically and otherwise. Many channelled messages point this out in earnest.

Since we are being invited into the Cosmic Network as new *members* we might care to dwell on what we have to offer. However, this will arise naturally as a part of our unfoldment.

It remains with us to act appropriately for the times and situation, and for each one of us to evolve our efforts out of the current needs.

Some of the changes ahead:

(1) Politically: the world will disarm through mutually acceptable negotiations based on the common need for survival. As co-operation and understanding unfold the best of East and West will be merged to form a new political order— acceptable to all, and seen as entirely viable and desirable.

(2) Mystically: all past and present forms of genuine mysticism will be reviewed and inter-blended where useful— leading to a new type of revelation: the synergical Cosmic View.

(3) Philosophically: resources will be distributed in such a way as to benefit all; world-wide communications will ensure that each and all will have a chance to measure needs accurately.

(4) Harmonically: all types of conflicts of interest will be resolved into a new sense of harmony; arts will flourish to express a state of being free of fear. A new cultural expression will arise, expressing the beauty of freedom.

(5) Scientifically: the inter-blending of all scientific knowledge will lead to discoveries which will permit science to make giant leaps towards establishing advanced appropriate technologies which are not at odds with the natural world (e.g., energy-producing generators will be pollution-free; natural resources will be endlessly recycled; healing therapies will no longer create damaging side-effects; the abuse perpetrated on animals used for research purposes will cease, and become replaced by accurate computerised simulations; etc.).

(6) Idealistically: advanced ideas will be blended, and result in a flexible idealism based on insight, and not on dogma. Religions will become free of doctrinal nonsense.

(7) Magickally: the appropriate ways of invoking creative devas will be understood, and this will lead to human-devic co-operation which in turn will bring about considerable changes in all the other domains of human life.

As humans start to expand into space and other dimensions of being, humanity as a whole will be able to explore itself in ways which so far have not been possible. Each new situation encountered will lead to new discoveries and new realisations. The possibilities are as exotic as they are endless...

JOURNEYING
— A WAY OF SELF-DISCOVERY

PRELUDE

Every now and then we witness the emergence of a new approach to psychic exploration — one which makes things easier of access and easier to relate to, intuitively and intellectually.

JOURNEYING — A WAY OF SELF-DISCOVERY may well be just such an approach.

This book outlines a method which, to the best of our knowledge, has never been set out in print before; and although it is a small book its scope is exciting, if not vast — as you will see for yourself.

It is also non-denominational — that is anyone or any group can use it, regardless of personal beliefs... unless those beliefs are far too dogmatic to make the use of it possible. As a method it can also be customised and integrated into what you are already doing by way of psychic exploration, or what you are familiar with. It can be seen as a way of self-discovery, a Spiritual connection path, a creative aid, and in some manner it can also be used in healing and therapy.

In the introduction the author explains something of its genesis, based as it was on meditation and consciousness projection over a period of almost 19 years (at the time), and actuated by a series of workshops during 1985 and 1986.

Then the method is set out as a series of sequential sections, which highlight certain areas which need to be understood singly as well as in their overall context. Finally there is much additional information which is given towards the end of this book to illustrate not only the possibilities ahead, but also to clarify issues related to the Cosmic domain.

We hope you will enjoy it and find it of great benefit.

0 — INTRODUCTION

JOURNEYING — A WAY OF SELF-DISCOVERY — is a preliminary document on a method which has been derived from workshop explorations over a period of 17 months; these workshops have mostly taken place at the Glastonbury Camps (1985 & 1986), and the method itself is still in the process of being further developed.

It all started with a workshop on Astral Projection where I was attempting to teach a number of people to project their consciousness out of their physical bodies using what is commonly referred to as their astral bodies, using visualisation as a key method. I told those participating what to expect, and what could happen. I told them about some of my own projections out of the body (over about 19 years at the time). I attempted to give them a framework in which to work — i.e. a way of assimilating this information intellectually — and I encouraged them to use their intuition as fully as possible.

The first two workshops of this kind were very much appreciated by those who participated, nevertheless it was obvious to me that it was difficult to teach a whole group of different individuals all at once; on a one-to-one basis the chances of success are far greater. I needed to find a different approach.

I started to evolve the idea of taking people on guided *journeys* instead, using a combination of methods, including visualisation and meditation. During the 2nd Glastonbury Living Astrology Camp (August 1985) I initiated two such journeys — the first to the Sun, Vulcan, Mercury and Venus; and the second to Mars, Jupiter, Saturn and Chiron.

The results were very encouraging. I had totally improvised the whole thing, allowing images to come to my mind spontaneously. Previously I had spent many years writing down subtle transmissions or channellings, and now I could see the link between these and guided journeys. The symbolic content of the journeys we had just done was very high; I began to perceive this as a different form of channelling.

It became obvious to me that in order to *activate* these journeys properly the journeying group needed to be *primed* beforehand. The first stage required a period of complete relaxation, as would be necessary if one was to project astrally out of the body, immediately followed by a second stage which provided a *vehicle* for the group — later we experimented with *spaceships,* and then with *bubbles of blue light* — which format turned out to be more popular. Simultaneously certain psychic safeguards were initiated to ensure that during moments of high sensitivity, especially when exploring exotic or alien *spaces*, no one would feel unduly threatened or at risk. The third stage consisted of the journey itself.

The result was a form of mental projection; at least this is one way of describing it, for technically it was not quite that. In fact the actual experiences invoked a variety of conceptual, symbolic and psychic-Spiritual perspectives, including alignments with higher energy sources, and different individuals tuned in to different areas of consciousness or *Plane* levels.

Subsequent journeys were undertaken to Uranus, Neptune, Pluto, and Alpha Centauri — which was our first *visit* to a location outside the Solar System. Following this we undertook a journey to the seven proto-suns, or Seven Sisters of the Pleiades, and this turned out to be a vital experience for several people; then the next day we went to Sirius *A* where certain symbolic *gates* were presented to us in order to access another universe via Sirius *B* — a *black hole* which we negotiated in perfect safety and equanimity by travelling through the *calm zone* down its magnetic axis; the group was then taken to a planet in that universe where, amongst other things, certain *keys* were given to those who were alert enough to invoke them and use them. The following journey took us to the centre of the galaxy, where the Universal Oneness was invoked, and then on to a planet in the Andromeda galaxy (M31/NGC224) — and here we entered an enormous conical Temple, from which no one seemed willing to return! It was a very moving, very deep experience for the participants, including myself as a channel — we had been surrounded by the power of several Spirit Tribes who had held the energy for us and protected and guided us for the whole duration of that session.

The amount of energy involved was tremendous; I myself experienced an open state of Kundalini for the whole length of that particular journey, and I found certain moments a bit difficult, because the energies that were being focused through me were very potent and I felt very responsible on behalf of the whole group. I could see various energy patterns of varying quality and *density,* some of which I could identify in terms that were familiar to me, while others I could not, nor did I feel a need to; since we were surrounded at the Camp by other on-going events there was a certain amount of physical sound interference; and to top that there was a certain amount of psychic interference as well, which had to be *filtered* out very consciously. It was a bit like holding on to the reins of a wild horse, yet riding it as fluently and as flowingly as possible. As I relaxed into the channelling and trusted the Spirit Tribes — which I could see at a subjective level — the resonance of my voice began to change. I then found it much easier to *ride* that wild horse, and the quality of the experience flowered into something even more powerful. It became an effortless process, and all I had to do was flow with it; I felt an overwhelming sense of Love. And the Temple itself, on that far-away Andromedan planet, is one of my favourite places.

Undoubtedly the journey could have gone on for a lot longer, which was substantiated by the fact that those present were very reluctant to come out of that state. As I brought people back to Earth and helped them to readapt to a lower order of consciousness and reality they remained unmoving in meditation, even with their eyes fully open. Eventually some of them got up slowly, moved around as if in a trance, though very conscious, thanked me or hugged me, and departed into the night, one by one...

except for one young man — who had joined the group over ten minutes late, and had therefore missed all the initial *programming* — he remained entirely still, lying on his back, his face very serene, as if in a deep sleep. At two or three minute intervals I shook him gently, but he would not come *back*. After about twenty-five minutes I called his spirit more directly, but he still would not come back. I did not want to leave him in that space, because the energies were changing, and I could feel elementals of a different order reasserting themselves bit by bit on that environment. I started talking to his subconscious mind, and then he came back very quickly. He was amazed that he had fallen asleep so deeply, and we talked for awhile. He had gone to a city during the day and come back to the Camp towards evening, and his energies had been somewhat less than harmonious. I helped him to close down his chakras and told him what he could do should he feel the need to do so — this is a very important part of any guided journey since many people do not really know how to close themselves down after being in a high psychic to Spiritual state of consciousness. Although he had been asleep almost throughout the whole session I knew very well that he had travelled in his subconscious state, and therefore that he was potentially vulnerable and needed added support.

I have been asked by several people what I would do if someone did not come back (and this also in relationship to Astral Projection). This was my first experience of someone who was really *sticking*. I didn't feel alarmed, even if I was concerned, but I also knew from my own experience over almost two decades that one always does come back. I have heard of rumours of *accidents* where this has not been the case, yet anyone involved in these areas of exploration has to trust the guiding forces which support these adventures into the higher states. What they can do from their side of things is considerably more than what anyone of us can do during incarnation. This is also why psychic sensitivity and a high degree of intuition are very important if one is to guide others on psychic journeys of any kind. I did not feel that he was at risk, therefore I did not have to take any drastic measures to bring him back; the process could be gentle. If I did not have that sensitivity I would not know that, but then nor would I be able to act as a channel.

At the last (Living Dance) Camp on request I led two more journeys — this time to hypothetical planets — one concerned with art and creativity, and the other with healing. In both cases *keys* were made accessible, and although I found hypothetical planets a lot less interesting to deal with as distinct from *real* ones, when I was told the next day by some of the participants that they had experienced healing, for instance, it showed us the potential of such ventures.

This manual must be accepted as nothing more than a preliminary account of what is possible. In due course it will be followed up by a more comprehensive manual.

Vee Van Dam — Glastonbury, September 1986.

(Camps where these workshops took place were: the 1st Glastonbury Earth Mysteries Camp, Beltane 1985; the 2nd Glastonbury Living Astrological Camp, Lugnasad 1985; the 3rd Glastonbury Living Astrological Camp, July 1986; and the 2nd Glastonbury Living Dance Camp, Lugnasad 1986. The 1st Glastonbury Ceremonial Camp, Summer Solstice/Litha 1986, was also very instrumental in providing new insights for these journeys. I missed the 2nd Earth Mysteries Camp, Beltane/Chernobyl 1986; and only briefly attended the 1st Living Dance Camp, Lugnasad 1985.)

1 — WHAT IS JOURNEYING?

In one sense it is a guided visualisation, except that the channelling guidance occurs at several levels simultaneously. Part of the time the channelling is in audible form, and part of the time it is silent, but a lot else is happening. During the periods of vocal channelling the group is given direct guidance — what to do, where to go, and how to get there. During the silent periods the guidance is in energy form and is subject to the subtleties of individual interpretation.

Insofar as any given individual is tuned in to the channelling, then that individual gets as much out of the experience as s/he is in a position to accept, absorb, and use. In a sentence, the more an individual is in any way enlightened or sensitive, the more s/he will get out of the process.

Therefore journeying is flexible. It can allow for the fact that a mixed group is not going to be composed of equally sensitive or perceptive individuals — each person gets what s/he needs. Effectively, s/he filters out that which s/he cannot cope with.

Above all else journeying is a method of facilitating *alignments* i.e. more or less direct transmissions of energies and impressions between higher Spiritual sources and the individuals who are *aligning* themselves consciously with those Spiritual sources.

The channel is something of a *lens* through which those transmissions are transmitted.

2 — THE DIFFERENCE BETWEEN JOURNEYING AND IMAGING

By way of distinction, imaging is a guided visualisation which accesses the subconscious mind. It facilitates the revelation of what is contained within that subconscious mind. It is largely an internal mental process, and is not normally subject to any transmission of energies or impressions from a higher Spiritual source(s). Much if not all the contents of an individual's subconscious mind are encoded in patterns of energy which were derived from past experience, from the current life, and from other lives or incarnations.

3 — PSYCHIC PROTECTION AT THE OUTSET OF A JOURNEY

When dealing with psychic currents of energy it is important to protect oneself. In the case of a journeying group the channel must facilitate or help create the *bubble of protection* which will offset any intrusions by undesirable psychic influences; this protective *bubble* or *shield* will also attenuate the impact of higher Spiritual and psychic energies, thus ensuring that no one becomes unduly overwhelmed by these.

The most dynamic protective device is a sphere, which when invoked is formed out of etheric energies; and blue light appears to be the most useful colour associated with psychic protection. Therefore invoking the parameters of the protective *bubble* can take the following form:

"Around you (the group) there is a circle; this circle defines the outer rim of a sphere of blue light which extends itself above you and below you. See this sphere of blue light as clearly as you can, and feel the protective quality of the blue light..."

In addition to this the channel can invite the participants to breathe in the blue light, until their whole bodies are thoroughly suffused with its radiance.

Other protective devices can be invoked: for instance, a cross of white light within the horizontal circle. Others might prefer to use a pentagram, or even define and consecrate the circle in advance by placing a long rope all around the journeying area — this rope should only be used for this purpose. Special items which have a protective quality may be placed within the circle, and these can be placed either within its centre, or else in a patterned shape (such as a cross, or a pentagram) within the circle.

It is largely up to the channel to decide what configuration of protection is most required for a particular journey. The protection itself is both symbolic and psychological, as well as actual and subjective.

4 — PSYCHIC PROTECTION DURING A JOURNEY

The channel may feel inspired to remind the group that it is in a protective environment, and this at intervals during a journey. In addition, particularly if the energies being drawn to the group are becoming very strong and are in some way upsetting the possible balance of this group, or else in any way endangering the balance of any given individual (it is up to the channel to ascertain whether this is so or not), the channel can and should take appropriate measures to counteract any excess of psychic pressure. This can be done in two principle ways: 1) by issuing specific words of advice; 2) by silently sending and surrounding individuals most at risk by coloured energies which are protective; these energies can be summoned by the channel through hir crown, ajna (third eye), or heart chakras, as appropriate. A third way, which can be used with the above two, is to project a protective symbol on the individuals concerned. A fourth way is to resonate a word of power or a mantra at a subvocal (or vocal) level which will have the effect of patterning the invoked energy and qualifying it with a particular effect (such as "harmony", "balance", "flow", etc., or with a word of power which is more group-specific according to one's magickal tradition).

5 — PSYCHIC PROTECTION AT THE END OF A JOURNEY

At the end of a journey it is important to bring the group *back to Earth,* and to make sure that each and all close down their chakric sensitivities. After a period of immersion in higher states of energy each individual will need to be *grounded* so that s/he will not feel unnecessarily exposed or vulnerable after the group has disbanded. To walk out of a group experience of this kind without taking these precautions could lead to disorientation, or even to psychic attacks. It is also a fact that during and after such sessions individuals may experience a powerful stimulation of their chakric centres, which in turn can lead to disturbing or even painful experiences around those power points — particularly the crown, ajna, heart and solar plexus. The whole or part(s) of their bodies may feel as if *on fire*, or *magnetised*, or *electrified*, or else they may associate their unease with an over-stimulation of their nervous system, either in a localised manner, or in a general sense. From one point of view this is normal and not as unhealthy as it might otherwise seem; any state or experience of accelerated evolution can engender these effects. From another point of view it could bring about much which is not at all desirable, such as periodic or even chronic energy turbulence, which in turn could make those individuals vulnerable and sensitive to all manner of environmental energy disturbances, or worse yet subject to the negative influence of entities which are not renown for their kindly disposition towards human beings, or evolutionary life in general.

See sections 31, 32 and 33 for extra details. Also Section 3 of THE PSYCHIC EXPLORER, in JOURNEYS BEYOND THE BODY: THE DIFFICULTIES OF ASTRAL PROJECTION; and various passages in INITIATION, TRANSMUTATION & IMMORTALITY.

6 — *THE CHOICE OF A JOURNEYING* TARGET

A journeying *target* is any location in space which is chosen for a journey. There are certain locations — associated with certain planets and stars, or even constellations of stars (keeping in mind that a constellation is a largely arbitrary grouping of stars within a certain vector of space) — which are in affinity or else working in association with the Earth as a planetary evolution, and with the Solar System as a whole. These are: all the planets of the Solar System; the Zodiacal constellations; the Pleiades, Sirius, Ursa Major, Polaris (veiling an unknown etheric stellar source), and a great many others. The Andromeda galaxy (ast. ref. M31/NGC224) is also a potent and yet largely undocumented source of affinitive energy.

In principle there is no limit as to what may constitute a *target*; nevertheless it would seem irrelevant to *visit* systems which have no or little bearing on the Earth's evolution, and it some cases it would probably be undesirable to make conscious contact with stellar sources which are not directly involved with the local cosmic evolution.

Further hints with regard to affinitive and associated stellar sources can be found in ESOTERIC ASTROLOGY (Alice A. Bailey; Lucis Press).

It is up to the channel to intuit with regard to a suitable target, yet the group should also feel free to make a specific request, including the choice of a hypothetical planet (associated with healing, creative potential, etc.) — and then it is up to the channel to ascertain intuitively if that request can and should be activated.

7 — SPIRITUAL & PSYCHIC ALIGNMENTS DURING JOURNEYS

In principle a Spiritual and psychic *alignment* is any method which brings about a direct or semi-direct contact with any given Spiritual source of energy and information. It is an invocation of that source, and the energies can then be directly (and sometimes indirectly) accessed. The experiences which may ensue will also be direct, semi-direct, or indirect, and may range from visionary to symbolic; those who cannot tune in directly may experience fantasies instead.

8 — THE CHANNELLING ELEMENT IN JOURNEYING

By definition a channel is anyone who, while in a state of heightened consciousness, can access a source(s) of Spiritual energies and information. Generally transmissions are received as impulses, which the channel then *translates* via hir brain into a form which can be communicated to others in a manner which will be understood.

In the case of journeying the channelling is a bit more complex, for the channel may perceive several overlapping impressions, and these may emanate from several levels, or Planes simultaneously. The channel not only invokes, focuses and then disseminates the information which is forthcoming, but must also remain sensitive to the state of being of all those present — i.e. the journeying group, and those who are *unseen* who may be holding the energy on behalf of the group. In addition to this s/he will have to screen out any undesirable influences by negating their impact — primarily by refusing to give them any conscious consideration, or even unconscious consideration; and above all else by refusing to channel in their unwanted energies.

The channel may receive the information not only as impulses and as qualities of energies, but also as symbolic codes — especially symbols which are akin to a universal language at a psychic and Spiritual level. During the course of a journey many such symbols may be encountered, particularly in a *target* area. The channel then has to decide — on an intuitive basis — which of these symbols should be revealed to the group, i.e. which are meant for group consumption, and which are designed only as pointers for the channel.

Therefore the channel is in a position of great responsibility and sensitivity, and must cope not only with the channelling itself, and overseeing the group and individual response, keeping an eye on what is being either called in and/or what is coming in of its own accord, screening out undesirable influences, interpreting the energies, the information and the symbols, etc., but must also *take the charge* of the focused energies. At its peak the process can be electric in its impact, and is often magnetic; a sensation of heat is almost always present. The incoming energies can invoke the channel's own Kundalini power, and vice-versa. The channel must be capable of balancing all these different aspects of a journey, and more besides. In consequence it is not advisable to activate a journey unless one is well trained and quite resilient and resourceful with regard to the kind of energies which can be accessed or encountered.

Journeying is not a game. It is a method which should be treated as one would any other magickal process — i.e. with respect, with love, with intuition, and with intelligence.

Should a channel find himself in difficulty s/he must do everything in hir power to maintain coherency and stability. The effect of not being able to do this could be detrimental not only to himself, but also to the whole group — with unknown consequences attached.

The purpose of the *overshadowing* (i.e. *unseen*) group is to take note of a channel's (and group's) condition and response, and to moderate the incoming energies accordingly. Thus the energies are transmitted through a chain of receivers-transmitters, and this all the way down the various Planes which may be involved.

9 — *THE COMBINED ENERGY OF A JOURNEYING GROUP*

Each individual participant in a journeying group represents a certain type and quality of energy, regardless of whether this individual is conscious of this or not. We are all Spiritual beings, and we are all evolving according to a pattern which is determined by, a) the soul element of our overall Self, and b) our Monad(s) (see note below). Our souls, from one angle of view, are Spiritual independent beings who nevertheless act within the periphery of influence of various soul groups; our souls are mediators between our Monad(s) (Cosmic Self), and our personality selves. Each soul has its own particular evolutionary designs within the purpose of the soul group to which it is attached or with which it is associated (it may be associated with more than one soul group). Our Monads, however, are One — i.e. there is only One Monad — nevertheless this One Monad (Cosmic Self, acting from the vantage of the Monadic Plane) is differentiated into a great multitude of individual monads.

Initially that differentiation only exists *in potential;* later, as a matter of evolutionary course, it becomes actual as, 1) our souls bring about individualisation of the conscious fractions which they incarnate, then, 2) through the ages guide those fractions towards initiation, and eventually towards transcendence. At this point the lower personality selves are *perfected* and become consciously merged with the souls, which have become fused with the Monad(s); as a result the cycles of incarnation then come to an end, and greater Spiritual journeys lie ahead of those who have achieved this transcendence.

(If you are unfamiliar with the terms used above, and the underlying concepts and realities these represent, a list of useful books is provided towards the end of this booklet, preceded by a glossary of terms.)

With this in mind a journeying group is composed of individuals who represent various stages of soul unfoldment, as the souls involved overshadow their respective incarnated fractions; collectively this represents a certain power to invoke higher Spiritual energies in line and in accordance with the needs of those souls involved. The combined energy of a journeying group can therefore be quite considerable, and the more the individuals involved are capable of heightened states of consciousness, the more this power for invocation will bring about access to higher levels of impressions and information.

Ideally a journeying group should be composed of individuals of roughly the same Spiritual *status* or unfoldment. When this is not the case those who are less conscious limit the full potential of the journeying experience, while those who are more conscious *pull* the less conscious into a higher state of consciousness. This can and almost always does work out to advantage. A balance is usually achieved, and each individual gets what s/he needs.

In the case of a group which meets regularly the actual heights which could be accessed could be quite staggering, and could prompt and advance individual and group unfoldment into areas which have not yet been documented outside of the circles of the Mystery Schools and certain shamanic groups.

10 — JOURNEYING FROM THE POINT OF VIEW OF A CHANNEL

The actual subjective experience of journeying varies from session to session, and this both for the channel as well as the journeying group. Not all journeys will seem dramatic, either in their contents or in their effects.

This will depend chiefly on three inter-related factors: the state of consciousness of the channel; the state of consciousness of the journeying group; and the response from the *unseen* side, or *unseen* support/channelling group(s).

At a minimal level the journeying experience — from the point of view of the channel — will be fairly easy going and consist of little more than a guided visualisation. This in itself may be quite adequate, and be as much as the journeying group involved can or will want to experience.

At a *maximum* level (keeping in mind that no specific *maximum* level can yet be defined) the experience will involve a lot of energy and a much higher state of consciousness — this may produce some stress for the channel, but may not necessarily put any great stress on the journeying group; each individual will essentially only *take in* what s/he needs or can accept and absorb.

Generally most journeys will fall somewhere between these two extremes, and what the channel may experience by way of duress will not normally be communicated in any manner to the journeying group itself. The channel generally takes the brunt of the power, but this has already been attenuated by the *unseen* overshadowing group. From moment to moment the extent of the power involved may change, nevertheless the overshadowing group will be taking this into account and making it safe enough to deal with. In electronic terms, by way of analogy, the overshadowing group plays something of the role of a mains filter, and reduces any peaks of electrical power to a more normalised supply.

11 — JOURNEYING FROM THE POINT OF VIEW OF THE GROUP

In a relaxed state each individual of the journeying group follows the guidance issued through the channel; nevertheless at any given interval an individual may drift off or lose hir conscious attention, or in some cases even fall asleep, and may or may not *rejoin* the journey at various points. This is fine. Some people will elect to subconsciously *phase in and out* in this way, while others will focus all their attention on the journeying experience throughout its whole duration.

Again, each individual gets what s/he needs — no more and no less. Even if s/he comes into the experience refreshed and alert, the subjective energies may alter hir state of receptivity and consciousness — producing either heightened awareness, or a lessening of sensitivity. In this lies a very useful safeguard: a channel must be aware of the whole group, and can only give a certain amount of support to any one given individual at any one time. Since the individual's experience is largely self-expanding and self-limiting the channel is free to do what s/he is best at doing: channelling. If this was not so one single individual could upset the whole journey for the rest of the group, and inhibit, or even worse, prevent, the full unfoldment of that journey. That is not to say that an individual's response may not or will not alter the distribution and quality of the energies present — for *good* or for *bad* — nevertheless each individual is insulated against any extremes of response that another or others might generate or manifest.

When dealing with psychic events of this type there must be a strong element of trust, although this would not excuse any foolhardiness, especially on the part of the channel. In one sense the channel is something of an *opener of gates,* permitting the group, or any individuals within the group, to access what is on the other side of those gates. Therefore the channel is a facilitator. Nevertheless each individual within the group can be in turn a facilitator on behalf of the others, primarily by being responsible for hir own responses or reactions. If everyone works the energies well, then everyone benefits greatly from that experience.

At no point should the channel open doors which s/he senses would be too dangerous; yet once stimulated any given individual can open a personal door for hirself, without adversely affecting the well-being of anyone else. Within the overall context of a single journey there is plenty of room for several individual journeys; each person is free to do whatever s/he chooses, and *go* wherever s/he pleases — although s/he may miss certain opportunities afforded by a closer attention being paid to the channelling information.

12 — INVOKING THE ONENESS OF THE JOURNEYING GROUP

One of the aims of journeying is to bring about a certain *atmosphere* and situation which everyone can share in common, and this regardless of any side-tracks which an individual many wish to explore. At the outset of a journey the channel is well advised to call upon the *Oneness* of the group, and this both symbolically and Spiritually, as well as practically. The more the group is united in its consciousness, the more there is a feeling of companionship and mutual support; this permits each individual to feel safe to explore with all the others present. It is often the case that each individual's experience is complementary to that of the others; in other words each person sees the journey from a different vantage point, yet it is the same journey which is seen by all.

This in itself allows for a lot of flexibility, and it also means that the overall information retrieved by the group is far more extensive than if everyone was to experience exactly the same thing. For a start some will be tuned more visually to the journey, whereas others will feel things instead; some may even have audio-like experiences. When sharing later it is often fascinating to realise that each person has a piece of a much bigger jig-saw puzzle. There are occasions, however, when the pieces do not seem to be very related, and no overall picture can be seen (which does not mean it is not there).

Invoking the *Oneness* of the group is also a very pertinent reminder that we are all essentially One Single Being — this is a fact of Spiritual Life; it is not a religious doctrine, or a philosophical concept. We are commenting here on the Cosmic Self as the underlying Cause of all manifestation, and while many people would wish to argue that either no such Being exists, or that this is the province of religion, from a much more pertinent angle it is *a state of Realisation;* even of sophistication. It has nothing to do with emotionalism or cultish aberrations; and the channel is not a priest or a priestess. It is not hir right to pass judgement on anyone or anything. Hir role is only to open up a door(s) for others, a door which s/he may have gone through hirself many times before, or maybe not as the case may be.

While a channel may know many things which would be considered abstract, it does not exclude the fact that within the journeying group there may be others who also know many things, and who may be equally adept in the channelling department. Again this may or may not be the case; and from another point of view at any one time we are all channels for something, even if this turns out to be nothing more than our own personal creativity, ingenuity, or even business sense. The term will be undoubtedly new and unfamiliar to many people, and it may be viewed with suspicion by others, and confusion may arise as to the true nature of channelling. One thing is sure: it does, or it can work, and this in a very creative and positive way; and what is more it can work equally well for different people with different backgrounds, and with different personal beliefs or aspirations. It has nothing to do with any set of beliefs in itself.

It should be obvious that the term *channel* is just a word; it is vaguely descriptive of the function which we are considering, and there is no doubt that many other words could be used as substitutes. In the sense that we are all channels, in some way or fashion, we are all inherently equal, yet there is no excuse for someone who *plays* at being a channel in a group situation without knowing what s/he is doing (it is also true to say that some people call themselves channels who do a fine job of externalising the contents of their own muddled subconscious!).

Also — given the realisation that we are all One Being in essence — we deserve to give each other support, and this especially during a group journeying session. At other times we may be too involved with our various personality differences to really appreciate the true import of this Oneness of Being, although it is always there, and this regardless of whether we acknowledge it or not at a continuous conscious level.

This is another, and very important, part of the journeying experience: it can unify people in consciousness. As a result of this it does put the onus on each and all of us to consider the true issues that we face as a humanity, and not to be divided by our attitudes. It is the way that we are inter-related which is important, rather than the way we are divided; and it matters not which kind of politics or religion, or philosophy we espouse, because none of these are intrinsically essential. Realisation of our fundamental Oneness, however, is.

We all use words. We all deal with concepts; and we all confound ourselves with patterns of thoughts and emotions at least part of the time. What happens when we are silent enough to realise that there is an undercurrent of pure telepathy between all parts of life, including ourselves? Journeying is one step towards answering that!

13 — PSYCHIC INTERFERENCE

Psychic interference can come in many ways and forms, some of these constituting direct interference, and others being more subtle. It is often difficult to assess exactly *what* is behind that interference, nevertheless generally speaking it is anything which could prove disruptive or counter-productive to a journey.

Given a situation where people are involved in an activity which is psychically sensitive, and especially if it is powerful, it is easy to imagine the amount of *light* which is generated. This is bound to attract attention on other levels, and maybe draw what may seem like undesirable entities or forces. In the strict sense most of these will not be malevolent; they may be elementals which occupy a certain area which do not feel at ease coping with a sudden stirring of higher energies. Their presence and effect can be harmonised, or a certain balance between their energies and the higher energies being channelled or generated can be achieved.

On the more serious front it is possible to draw negative influences which are adverse to manifestations of Light; these must be denied any access to the group working, and it is up to the overshadowing group and the channel to ensure that this is denial is maintained.

This is why a properly consecrated working space is not only advisable but essential, and why the psychic protection invoked at the beginning of a journey is necessary. On the lower planes of existence Light is almost always attended by manifestations of darkness, since these planes are subject to duality (whereas the higher Planes are not; they are the expression of Unity and Union). This is a factor which we have to bear with every day of our lives regardless of whether we are directly conscious of it or not. The Light pulls us one way, and the darkness the other, and we are given the choice to decide where we want to place our allegiance.

From another point of view there is no such division: all Life is Power — the Power-to-Be, the Power-to-Love, and the Power-to-Create. If we were not pulled simultaneously or alternatively by what we may think of as Light and darkness (or evolutionary and involutionary forces) we would not evolve a sense of balance; and it is *balance* which is of vital importance in the end analysis. To be in-balance is to unify what is otherwise separated by the mind: the forces which draw upwards, and the forces which draw downwards. By becoming masters of *balancing* we can move up and down at will, and no longer participate in the relative illusion of separation.

During a journey this need for balance is very important, and it is a great lesson to learn how to be in-balance. It is not easy, yet it is also not impossible. We all embody positive and negative energies, and when we learn how to keep ourselves in balance we are no longer adversely affected by the interplay between the two.

When the twin polarity of nature is understood, and the evolutionary and involutionary principle are considered in their rightful place, then there is no dualism. They are part of a whole; they each have their part to play in the drama of manifestation; and we, being subject to both their influences, have to find out how to cope with both, rather than being afraid or unduly hindered by their interplay.

Invoking positive power breeds positive results in journeying, however.

14 — *THE BEGINNING OF A JOURNEY*

At the outset of a journey the group is given an imaginary environment to work with and from: for instance, a *bubble of light*, or a *spaceship*. This environment then becomes a vehicle for that journey.

The channel then invites the journeyers to perceive themselves rising off the Earth and away from their physical surroundings, and then to see themselves travelling through space towards the target area. The actual form that this initial stage of the journey will take will depend on the channelling itself.

(Alternatively the channel can take people straight to a given target, or to any other point in space.)

15 — *THE UNFOLDMENT OF A JOURNEY*

From here onwards there are no set rules or regulations. The channelling will determine the exact nature of the appropriate visualisation to be held. As the journey unfolds the participants may be taken through a number of *steps* which will permit them to adapt to that journey, and eventually to the nature of the target area.

It is important to understand that the channel is journeying too. S/he will not be able to relax in quite the same way as the other participants since s/he has to cope with many things which the others do not have to bother themselves with. Nevertheless s/he is discovering and learning as well, and s/he will be required to adapt much faster than the others since s/he is effectively in the *pilot's seat* — even if s/he is being guided hirself by higher influences. S/he has to make intuitive decisions based on a two-way input-output perception of the situation; s/he has to decide what to channel in, and what to leave out, or else keep out; and s/he needs to keep hirself open to higher impressions while giving out directions.

At any one time s/he may see that a given individual, or even the whole group, needs a specific input of information. At a very immediate level s/he will have to ask of the higher influences what is to be done, or s/he may know what to do anyway; and s/he will have to act accordingly, see or feel the results, and then amend and/or request for further advice or clarification if such is necessary.

In all this s/he must be as clear as s/he can be, and there is sometimes little margin for error — not because a bad decision will necessarily lead to any disaster, but because any inappropriate decision will hamper the flow and unfoldment of the journey — it is important to flow as much as is possible, and not to jar the participants with inadequate information or energies.

Anyone who is involved in these areas of psychic and Spiritual discoveries can learn to channel on these terms. It is an art, and it is also a science.

16 — THE CHOICE OF DOORWAYS

A psychic *doorway* usually comes in the form of a symbol; it may be a circle, a triangle, or some other geometric design, or it may be less abstract and actually look like a door, a gate, or the entrance to a tunnel, etc. The *doorway* may have a specific colour or else may radiate a specific quality of light; or it may be matt black (which normally indicates a powerful place beyond, and also acts as a warning against the wrongful or inadequate approach and entry to that doorway). Many of these doorways will be found within specific yet often subjective locations — on a planet, within a star, and so on.

A doorway of this kind is usually a means of accessing another area which lies beyond it, and what lies beyond it may or may not be in the same spacial area — for instance, a doorway may be found within a given star which leads to another star, or to a planet, or to an abstract part of space; or to another level of existence. The extent to which an individual journeyer will be able to access that place in full consciousness will depend largely if not entirely on hir aptitude at a psychic and Spiritual level to integrate this experience. If s/he is not ready for a conscious contact and/or perception of that space or area s/he will not experience it, yet this in itself will not prevent hir from continuing with the journey or from deriving benefit from it. Many people who are not ready for these places *phase out* for awhile until the journey comes back to within their conscious reach; and if they find that where they are taken is not accessible to them as a whole they may phase out for the remainder of the journey, although they will usually at least rejoin it by the time of the return sequence. Conversely they may experience these areas in a lesser way, e.g. enter a stage of day-dreaming and fantasy, but they will miss out on the true significance involved and the opportunities offered — that is at a conscious level; at a subconscious level they will know what is happening/has happened, i.e. an internal level of their consciousness will see it clearly, whereas their outer consciousness may not (it may surface sometimes days, weeks, months, or even years later).

17 — APPROACHING A JOURNEYING TARGET

Allowing for the fact that a target area will almost always be somewhat alien in character the channel must bridge this alien factor with what may be familiar to the participants. Thus if the target is a planet in some other star system it is often best for hir to present it in simple terms, regardless of what s/he may perceive of it hirself. A general description of the whole planet can be given, and something of the quality of its energies can be imparted. The approach can be slow, or else it can be direct, fast, or nearly instantaneous.

Those who have already participated in many journeys may

prefer the latter approach, and thereby dispense with the preliminaries of approaching a target area, whereas newcomers to journeying may need a slower course of access.

With this in mind a channel must decide which of the two approaches is best for the whole group, and if there are newcomers participating alongside others who are more acquainted with the process of journeying it is generally advisable to adopt the slower approach — even if the others might prefer a more direct access.

18 — LANDING ON A JOURNEYING TARGET

Assuming that a slower approach is initiated the group can be given an overview of the planet (sunstar, etc.). The actual descent onto that planet can be progressive, and the group can be taken around the planet first while gradually approaching it, or it can be taken directly to a given area. The channel can point out features which may be of special interest.

The terrain encountered may be open, simple or complex, and this will depend on what the channel perceives hirself, or what s/he is given to pass on to the others by way of suggestions or specific images. If the place is relatively barren at first sight this is usually because there is something very special to be seen nearby — this may be a symbol, a particular feature, or a combination of both. The channel can draw attention to this, and to any colours or qualities of energies which may be present.

If there is a city then it is often best to land outside it, and then to invite the participants to walk into it through a given angle, gate, or avenue; or else the individuals within the group can be given the choice of how to enter this place.

If the area is in effect a *switchboard* to many other places, then the channel can give a description of the various places which can be accessed from this initial target and allow each individual to choose where they would like to go. When this is done the choice must be presented as quickly and as simply as possible, outlining first the number of places, and then giving out enough information with regard to each of these to permit the participants to make their choice; conversely, giving out too much information with regard to any one place will usually end up prompting everyone to go there, instead of waiting for other choices to be announced or described.

19 — EXPLORING A JOURNEYING TARGET

The exploration of a target will usually be described in a sequential manner, allowing for pauses so that each individual can develop hir own visualisation of that place and thereby perceive what s/he needs to make contact with. To rush the sequences will not permit the participants to do this.

In this the channel must be especially sensitive to the overall response of all the individuals present, and it is often not possible to cater for the needs of each person on a separate basis; some may wish to move on faster, and others may care to linger for a while in a certain area. This is a difficulty which must be taken into account, and the channel may elect to give people the choice to follow the main course of the journey, or else to go off exploring on their own account if such an approach seems desirable or of interest to them.

If a *switchboard* area has been encountered, and individuals each go off to places of their own choice, then the channel must allow people enough time to explore the secondary targets they have elected to explore. The channel may remain silent for a few minutes or for a longer period. S/he will also have to intuit as to whether s/he should issue *beacon calls* at intervals so that those who may feel uneasy about the lack of audible guidance will feel reassured that there is a central *rendez-vous* point to which they can come back if they feel the need to do so. "OM" sounds are often good for this purpose

The above does not cover all the possibilities which may arise, but it does at least give an idea of what may happen.

20 — INDIVIDUAL PERCEPTION

What each individual perceives and experiences during a journey depends not only on the channelling itself, but on that individual's ability to convert that channelling into visual and other sensory impressions — at least approximately. While the process may be of a psychic nature, it is also an invitation to simulate physical-like experiences through visualisation; on occasions the visualisation may be more abstract, however.

The degree to which any given individual is successful in doing this will determine how vividly s/he will experience the various elements of a journey. At best that experience can be quasi-real; at worst it will seem like a day-dream (unless s/he becomes unconscious); and generally speaking it will probably fall somewhere between these two possibilities.

While some elements of the journey may come across as fantasist, the important parts of that journey consist of any special experiences and of the interpretation of the symbols which may arise, and what these symbols may convey by way of information or by way of facility.

The channel can introduce the group to specific *keys* — for instance, by introducing a symbol which is described as a *key* to a particular skill; for example, one's own personal sense of creativity. This symbol then becomes a means of accessing one's own power of creativity during subsequent periods of meditation.

Keys are one of the high points of journeying. They can become *tools* which can then be used whenever they are required.

Some people have great difficulty in visualising things, therefore the channel must cater for these by invoking other possible perceptions: sounds, touch, words, etc. In this case a *key* could be a specific sound instead; and so on.

The channel can also introduce the group to guides who may *reside* at target areas; these guides will then introduce each individual to certain aspects of what can be learnt or accessed in those areas. Most people will visualise these guides in a great variety of different ways, and will be shown things of special interest to themselves individually.

21 — GROUP PERCEPTION

Whenever the whole group perceives a journey or else elements of a journey in common a new possibility comes into focus: group consciousness can actually precipitate a much greater sense of reality with regard to the experience of a journey, and ideally this is something which is very desirable as it could lead to types of consciousness projection which would elevate the whole art of journeying into a much higher domain.

For instance, an astral projector can access parts of the higher astral plane which are very real by way of experience; s/he will *know* that s/he is *there*. There is plenty of evidence from shamanic sources that group projection of this kind is possible.

On a more subjective level it is equally possible to access the higher Planes, such as the higher mental, buddhic, atmic, and monadic Planes. By subjective it is meant that the experience will be somewhat abstract, which in itself does not mean that it is not real. It can be immensely powerful.

We do appear to be entering an Age when these things will be accessible as a group, rather than as individuals, which has been generally the case so far. With this in mind a study of the books mentioned in the bibliography at the end of this book could prove very useful to you.

One of the results of the rapid unfoldment of the Aquarian Age, as inspired and influenced by the 7th Ray (of Magick), is that a much greater sense of planetary telepathy will be experienced by all those who are sufficiently sensitive to the *network* or *telepathic web*. This effect and reality is also being promoted by the increase of communication world-wide; and in this there is a clue as how we will overcome many of our problems, and why we are experiencing an increase in internal pressure as well.

22 — PERIODS OF SILENCE IN THE CHANNELLING

Although this point has already been mentioned it is pertinent to add that a channel is in a position to convey much which does not need to be expressed at an audible level. Subjectively the journey is an *alignment* between the recipients and the source(s) of influence; this source of influence in turn is in *alignment* with an even higher source; in this way a journeying group can become *aligned* to cosmic principles which are not easily accessed by a lone individual.

Words in themselves would be totally inadequate to express the full relevance or actuality of these *alignments,* therefore it will be during the moments of silence that much will be experienced. The channelled words can then be seen as promptings, upon which the silence can reveal the full extent of the power of a journey.

23 — PROMPTINGS

At specific moments the channel can introduce special directions which will key in the participants to equally special areas of contact. Each prompting initiates a period of access to a higher state of consciousness; and each such period is an *opening door* in itself.

Promptings can also be used to redirect the group, or certain individuals within the group, when the energies are being dissipated in some manner — usually because of lack of attention.

24 — THE INVOKING OF SPECIFIC SYMBOLIC KEYS

Certain symbols are fairly universal in their power and effect, and these have been recognised down the ages by all those who have been involved in subjective explorations. It is important to think of symbols as a type of advanced language one which can be used to bridge the gap in experience-reality between the human domain and the devic domain, and between these and higher orders of Reality.

Certain symbols — often quite complex in their structure — can be used to access certain *restricted* areas of higher consciousness, and at the discretion of the channel, and providing s/he is guided to reveal them in some way, even if only silently, these symbols can be invoked on behalf of the group. It would be totally inappropriate to reveal any of these symbols in print, since they must be *given* to a human recipient during moments of inner contact.

25 — THE END STAGE OF A JOURNEY

Towards the end of a journey the channel must call the participants back to a regroupment area, from which the group will then depart. It is important to give everyone enough time to do this; and some people usually need more time than others. The effect of being left behind somewhere can be a bit disconcerting to the individuals involved, and could cause them some difficulty in returning to the physical plane reality after a period of high contact.

The channel should also summarise — in some relevant way — what the journey has been about, if this seems pertinent. Time should be given to say goodbye to any guides, thus permitting a resolution of that particular form of contact. And the channel should remind everyone to say goodbye and give love to the target area, i.e. the place, the planet, or the sunstar, and to thank it for what it has revealed and shown of itself.

26 — RETURNING FROM A JOURNEY

The return should be comparatively swift; there is little point spending too much time in doing this — except when approaching the Earth and the original place of departure, whereupon the descent back to Earth should be reasonably gradual and visual (except in the case of an advanced journeying group, which will not need this, in which case the return can be relatively instantaneous). Coming in to *land* can be quite fun as well, although some people may feel that they did not really want to leave the target area!

27 — GROUNDING *A JOURNEY*

Then it remains with the channel to make sure that a reintegration into the physical plane reality and environment is induced. S/he should bring people back to this order of reality gently, yet firmly. The group's attention should be drawn to the initial area of departure, and reminded of the *bubble* of blue light. Then the channel should go through the procedure which will permit the closing down of the chakras — for instance, by prompting everyone to surround themselves with blue light, then tightening that blue light around their auras; then call upon them to seal their chakras with either circles, circle-crosses, pentagrams, or a combination of these, and this mentally, or by using the right hand in symbolic gesture.

28 — *MAKING SURE EVERYONE IS* BACK

Finally the channel should look around for those who have not yet reintegrated into the physical plane reality and then attend to them individually. Unless there is a good cause to do otherwise s/he should bring them back gently, yet again, firmly.

There may those who do not want to come back — either because they are enjoying their contact *elsewhere* and feel that they have not *finished* with what they are doing or experiencing there; or else because they are somewhat *stuck* there for some reason.

The channel then has to decide whether to call them back anyway, or to leave them to their own devices. If s/he knows, and *sees* or *feels,* that the individual or individuals concerned can *take care of themselves,* or else knows that they have a propensity for prolonging their inner Plane or subjective contacts, then s/he can let them be for awhile and address other matters instead. If on the other hand s/he *feels* (psychically, that is) that someone is stuck somewhere, then s/he needs to attend to that individual's particular needs — while also making sure that the rest of the group has *returned*, and that it is duly *grounding* its energies in an appropriate manner.

In practice these matters are rarely matters of concern; nevertheless, and ideally, and should the case be that more than one individual gets stuck *out there* — either at the target area or elsewhere — then if there are other participants who are sufficiently experienced to take over the role of calling them or guiding them back, so much the better — in a well integrated group, particularly one which has worked often as a magickal team, there should be at least a number of people who are quite able and sensitive enough to do what is necessary — nevertheless they should refer to the channel first before attempting to do this as the channel is likely to *see* things from a better perspective initially.

If the group, as a whole, is not quite that advanced yet, then the channel must *feel* and *see* the situation internally, take advice from the higher guiding sources, and then do whatever is necessary to ensure the safety of the individual or individuals concerned.

29 — SPECIAL CASES

Those participants who have already been delving into the higher states of existence for some while — even if only in deep meditation — will not normally have any difficulty in reintegrating their consciousness with physical plane conditions. For them the process will be relatively matter of fact.

Others who may not have explored these areas very widely may experience some difficulty in making the necessary adjustments, and these will have to be given advice and support. More importantly any experience of the higher states — in any form — tends to activate a process of purification, and if individuals harbour personal problems it may emphasise these problems by bringing them to the fore — either immediately, or else over the time ahead. In the immediate sense, after a journey, some people may feel a little overwhelmed by energies which they may find difficult to control or subdue. They may find themselves confronted by their own negativity, and this may be uncomfortable or even a little scary; and this may be further compounded by *holes* in their auras through which negative influences could have an unwelcomed impact.

It is important for a channel to assess this situation and to make sure that first of all those auric holes are closed up; secondly that these people are given the opportunity to talk about their difficulties so that solutions can be found to them; and thirdly that they do not depart from the group feeling vulnerable or unnecessarily exposed.

From one point of view these problems are the sort of things which are going to become evident as part of any personal growth, and they are not actually caused by the journey itself, although a journeying experience may activate them and make them come to the surface of consciousness. Problems of this kind are also evidence that personal healing is taking place.

If the journeying group is meeting regularly, then these problems can be ironed out over a period of time. If the group does not meet regularly, then these individuals must be able to reach the channel for advice, and/or else be put in contact with counsellors or therapists who deal with psychological *and* psychic problems (an ordinary psychologist or psychotherapist is not going to be of much use here).

In the main these matters will not constitute the sort of problems which cannot be dealt with within the circle of a group, and the above is mentioned as a safeguard. For many weeks, if not months after a journey, and especially a series of journeys, people can experience energies impinging on their chakras, which energies they may not feel able to deal with easily without advice and support. Should problems of this kind arise the channel should be prepared to visit these people at their homes, or else a special group session, or a number of sessions, should be arranged to tackle them upfront.

Actually feeling these energies is also a good sign that an acceleration of growth is taking place, and while that acceleration can cause difficulties it is not negative in itself. There are a number of ways of not only dealing with the manifestation of these energies, but also of using them to good advantage. With this in mind a course of journeys should be accompanied by a course in meditation and advanced psychic studies, include discussion sessions, and various methods of healing and creative visualisation should be explored as well, thus giving everyone the opportunity to deal with their problems and difficulties directly, with and without the support of others.

Also groups in any given area should meet reasonably regularly not only to assess and deal with any difficulties, but also to discuss the implications of journeying, etc., and this with the channel present at least occasionally.

If after a journey someone, or even several people, are in an unconscious state (i.e. out of their bodies or asleep) they will need to be brought back to wakeful consciousness — and this gently. The channel should call upon their spirits to return, and/or talk to their subconscious minds as may be appropriate. They should not be forced to return abruptly, since this could cause a certain degree of shock which could prove to be damaging in some circumstances. Only in very specific cases should the channel take whatever measures are necessary to bring someone back in a less gentle manner — for instance, by rolling that person from side to side, or, more dramatically, and availability permitting, by immersing hir in cold water (a shamanic practice which helps people to coalesce their various bodies — spiritual, mental, astral, etheric and physical).

This book does not attempt to cover all the possible events which may arise from an exposure to psychic energies and forces — much by way of useful information can be found in THE PSYCHIC EXPLORER, and in STARCRAFT.

30 — THE SHARING OF THE JOURNEYING EXPERIENCE

Individuals within a journeying group may wish to talk about their experiences after a journey, and the channel should encourage them (but not force them) to do so. Sharing insights is usually very rewarding since it brings back to memory events and experiences which otherwise could be forgotten, and it is often the case that one person, or several people, talking about their experiences will actually help others to remember events which took place, but which had already escaped their consciousness upon reintegrating it with the physical plane.

The sharing of the journeying experience can take as long as people may feel the need, and it often takes as long as the journey itself, and sometimes longer. It is often great fun and very revealing, as different people highlight the different episodes which they have experienced. Everyone can learn something from this sharing.

The channel should ask people questions and encourage the participants to remember their experiences more precisely, and where pertinent should offer supplementary explanations and answer any questions which may be forthcoming.

Those who feel so inclined can take notes for later reference.

It is also a good idea to have light snacks, cookies, fruit, and hot drinks readily available after a journey; this helps in grounding the energies.

31 — CLOSING DOWN THE CHAKRAS

The actual sharing of these experiences can reopen the chakras to a certain degree, and before the group disbands the channel should take everyone through a final period of closing them down again.

Different people employ different ideas and techniques with this in mind. Many of these techniques are based on psychological devices which help people to identify in a simple way with the process of closing down the chakras to a more normal level of activity. Other techniques work directly on the structure of the chakras, and most of these particular methods use symbolic movements of energy — either applied purely mentally, or else supported by hand movements.

A circle acts by *enclosing* the chakric energies within a given space; the circle really represents a sphere — therefore what an individual is doing by applying such a symbol is enclosing the chakras within a sphere of protective light. Each chakra should be enclosed separately, working from the crown chakra downwards, including the ajna (third eye), throat, heart, solar plexus, spleen, and the sexual and base chakras.

A cross harmonises the male and female elements of the chakric energies, and brings them into perfect balance. A combination of circle and cross protection is therefore very effective.

A pentagram addresses the elemental energies, and by moving the pentagram clockwise from apex to lower right, to upper left, through to upper right, to lower left, and back to the apex, actually seals the elemental energies (yet may also stimulate the chakras, particularly the ajna — nevertheless it is protective). A combination of circle, cross and pentagram protection is therefore even more effective.

Coloured energies (i.e. particular wavelengths of diffracted white light) can be used simultaneously, especially blue light, indigo and/or white. The following colours and their most prominent effects are listed here for reference:

VIOLET — Purifying; being a combination of blue and red it is both protective and stimulating. Violet is often used as an alternative to white light, especially in magickal applications.

INDIGO — Initiating; indigo is a combination where blue predominates, with a smaller proportion of red. It is often used for deep Spiritual contact where inner revelations are sought. Related to the intuition and the Spiritualised intellect.

BLUE — Protective; the best colour to use for protection in most circumstances. It has a *cooling,* soothing or stilling effect, and prevents energies from getting out of control. Very healing.

GREEN — Balancing; also soothing, it brings all energies into harmony with Nature. Being the complementary-opposite of red — and often used with blue — it is used extensively in colour healing.

YELLOW-GOLD — Stimulates the intellect, especially the higher intellect. Good for people who want to develop their minds or apply themselves in mental ways. Can be used with indigo to correlate the higher intellect with the intuition.

ORANGE — Stimulates the etheric (vital energy) counterpart of the physical body, and via that etheric counterpart the physical body itself. Used for general stimulation.

RED — Very stimulating; red is the longest wavelength of coloured light and as such it is somewhat unstable, and can be dangerous when applied without proper discrimination. In most cases rose-red is a safer colour to use.

These are the seven prismatic *rainbow* colours or diffractions of Primary White, which latter therefore embodies all their effects, in potential and in effect. Complementary-opposite colours are violet/indigo and yellow/gold, blue and orange, and green and red. Violet includes ultra-violet light (very short wavelengths), and red includes infra-red light (very long wavelengths).

An indication of the power of colours is revealed in the fact that if you expose a plant to red light it will grow very fast, very tall (for its species at least), and it will die very quickly; if you expose a similar plant to blue light it will grow very slowly, very stunted and spread, and it will remain alive for a long time. If you expose a person to a lot of red light s/he will feel initially very energised and stimulated, then become agitated and nervous, and finally may feel very tired, and may even break down mentally, emotionally, and/or physically; this is also the effect of positively charged or ionised particles. If you expose a person to blue light s/he will feel initially soothed, refreshed and protected, then become more and more still, and then may enter into a deep meditation; this is also the effect of negatively charged or ionised particles.

Obviously any excess of exposure to any colour may produce unwanted or undesirable effects.

32 — DISBANDING

When people leave after the conclusion of a journeying session they should be encouraged to think of themselves as surrounded by an aura of blue light. Energy follows mental input, and if they can visualise this clearly then they *will* be surrounded by that blue light. It is usually best to focus this protective blue light on the heart chakra, which has magnetic properties, and to move it with the ajna (third eye). This blue light will then filter out any external energies which could have an adverse effect, psychically, mentally, emotionally and etheric-physically; and it will also preserve the useful energies which have been sealed internally within their auras.

After a journey people should avoid any activities which are likely to be demanding or strenuous, and this for at least several hours. This does not mean that one should remain inactive, however. Also with more experience it becomes less inadvisable to pass from one activity, such as journeying, to another, such as driving, working, or involving oneself with relatively chaotic or demanding energies.

Before going to sleep they should go through the act of closing down their chakras once again, as an extra protection.

33 — THE LASTING EFFECTS OF JOURNEYING

Journeying is a creative process, and like all creative processes it requires a certain sensitivity and artistry to make it work for oneself, and for a group. Its applications are so wide-ranging that at this point it is far too early to comment on the fulness of its potential, yet it is obvious that it can be immensely inspiring and practical in its effect, and in theory at least it could be used to address almost anything — especially as it can provide people with *keys* or *tools* to work with.

Therefore it is an exciting way of self-discovery, and one

which can be used in conjunction with meditation and other methods of self-realisation; those who participated in the journeys undertaken so far (e.g. at the Glastonbury Camps), and who were alert enough to truly benefit from the experience, would undoubtedly attest to this.

The advantage of a system which allows each individual to make hir own special connections at an internal level should be self-evident: it is flexible, direct, and unbiased — i.e. it fulfils one's needs without the encumbrance of dogma, and this in itself should make it particularly attractive.

The positive effects of journeying can be long lasting since each individual can address hir Higher Self with an ever-greater measure of consciousness and realisation. Even someone who finds that addressing somewhat difficult initially will experience various benefits, directly and indirectly, and over a period of time.

34 — THE CREATIVE POTENTIAL OF JOURNEYING

Since journeying can unlock areas of the psychic and Spiritual worlds which lay often dormant and unrecognised, in theory at least there is nothing which journeying could not be used for. It is a means of accessing countless sources of specialised energies and information, and as such it can be immensely beneficial.

It allows for *customisation*. Given a group of people who might want to explore a specific area of their creativity, and this together, a suitable target can be chosen for this purpose. Let us say that a group of artists wanted to access a source or sources which might help them to unlock their talents further, the channel can *scan* the heavens or inner space for such a source(s), and then take the group there forthwith.

It is important to remember that the channel is a facilitator, and not a leader, or a priest/ess. The journeying group can thus discuss where they might want to go, or what they might want out of the journeying process, and the channel then can then look for and invoke an appropriate source of influence.

35 — THE SPIRITUAL SIGNIFICANCE AND USEFULNESS OF JOURNEYING

It is an unfortunate thing in some ways that Spirituality is so often associated with religion as it is more commonly understood. The Spirit within us all may inspire us to feel religious, nevertheless in itself it is not a religion. It is a particular state of Being, and of consciousness.

Journeying, above all else, is a *Spiritual alignment* — i.e. an *alignment* between the lower self and the Higher Self, and this to whatever variable extent. It can be used as a general introduction to the Spirit, or it can be used as a general method of Spiritual contact; at best it is a way of inducing Life-Initiations (as described in THE PSYCHIC EXPLORER).

If a group were to meet regularly to explore the potential of Spiritual contact through journeying one can imagine that not only much useful information would be gained, but that it might well prove to be an *access route to the stars* — i.e. to everything which different star systems embody by way of evolutionary energies and progress; in other words a group working together regularly could put themselves in contact with vital areas of interest, and would obviously experience fundamental personal and group changes accordingly. Projecting further one can imagine that the group would become more and more acquainted with what can only be called the Cosmic Network, and would become increasingly able with regard to accessing *any* part of that Network, within its range of evolving abilities at least.

The long term possibilities which this may afford are incalculable; we stand in this manner at the gate of a more or less entirely untapped avenue of Self and group realisation... untapped at least to the extent that a method such as journeying has not been used very much outside of the Mystery Schools and certain shamanic circles.

36 — HIGHER TYPES OF CONSCIOUSNESS PROJECTION

Journeying could lead to experiences which might be so vivid that they would put either individuals or the whole group in direct, living contact with higher levels of existence, or Planes. What these experiences might reveal by way of extra facilities with regard to the use of journeying methods... we will find out. This cannot be an intellectual process, since the Higher Planes are beyond the intellect — except for the Higher Mental Plane, which embodies the higher intellect.

Once sufficiently experienced a group of individuals may not need to meet physically before undertaking a journey. Those involved could depart from various physical locations and meet on higher levels. This would necessitate a high degree of telepathic ability and rapport, yet this is by no means out of the question. Then the journey could be facilitated by the channel from that vantage (i.e. from inner side), or else the whole group could find itself in a state of shared channelling. A speculative proposition, nevertheless it is a distinct possibility.

Before that could be achieved much journeying would have to be done by that group, which in turn would entail much by way of complementary activities of a psychic and Spiritual nature. Each individual within the group would have to be well advanced in hir abilities to project hir consciousness in a variety of ways, to various locations on various Planes, including *places* outside of space and time — and this not so much in a subjective manner but in a real way.

37 — TRANSCENDENCE THROUGH JOURNEYING

The *ultimate* question is can journeying lead to transcendence? And the answer appears to be "Yes!".

However, what should one understand by the word *transcendence?* For many of us the human world is the only world that we know of, consciously that is. Our assumptions with regard to the Universe at large are based on our human perceptions, and the extensions of our perceptions through technology. The immediate limitations of our physical technologies place even greater limitations on our perceptions, and therefore lead us to make what can only be called inadequate or partial assumptions — and this regardless of how aesthetic our scientific or conceptual theories may be at any one time.

Journeying, in one way, is possibly an entry point into mental, psychic and Spiritual *technologies* whereby we can tune into the Cosmos and derive new impressions — impressions which by virtue of their nature will pull us up into a greater area of consciousness, and this on an ever-increasing basis. This may be seen as a predictable evolutionary step, which once taken will lead us towards a recognition and acknowledgement of metaphysical realities and interconnections which have evolved around us in space, in our system and in other star systems — interconnections which have been made between intelligent and Spiritual races of varying evolutionary background.

The Cosmos, in one sense, is much like an expanded world. Within that world there are x amount of races and x amount of *countries*. Having evolved to the extent that an awareness of the Cosmic environment has been achieved then neighbours in space begin to communicate. The thread lines of that communication are rudimentary to begin with, yet within a certain time these are enhanced and expanded into a full Network — which before that time may have existed *in potential* anyway; certain standards are agreed upon, evolved from a close scrutiny of Nature/Supernature — involving an understanding of the creative forces which mould our Universe and that of other Universes. The encoding of the information passing along the lines of that Network are as universal as they can be, i.e. they are symbolic and energetic; transmission of energy encapsulates a coded symbology which can be *read* by any intelligence and consciousness which peers into the mysteries of Nature/Supernature. Each intelligence/consciousness has the potential for activating or for evolving the necessary *equipment* which will permit it to tune in to the Network and decipher the information, and then to transmit a response.

The symbolic information then becomes a means of inviting

a greater contact through the medium of direct telepathy, and where relevant the information is stepped down to allow the new *subscribers* to adapt to the nature of and operational principles involved in that Network. Since the potential for telepathic communication is infinite the Network is made up of *switchboards*, and in effect within that One Network there are many lesser networks — all acting on the same overall principles, yet each network also a function of a particular *framework*. Given the ability to link up with those networks which are closer (in relative terms) to the Cosmic Network, the notions and acknowledgement of Space and Time are transcended, and that awareness realises that:

1) Telepathy is not primarily transmitted from one point to another as mental thought-forms; telepathy is an *open state* of sharing between different foci of consciousness *beyond Space and Time*.

2) Each focus of consciousness is inherently Cosmic in nature, therefore has the potential for infinite communication.

3) Each focus of consciousness has limitations by virtue of its embodiment and expression within manifestation; and yet it is those limitations which facilitate the evolution of points of view which can be communicated and shared.

4) Conscious transcendence of the form aspect of expression leads to a greater sense of *Gestalt*, or Oneness with the Whole.

5) The highest form possible is an infinitely small point, counterbalanced by an infinitely great embodiment of manifestation — in other words to achieve infinite consciousness requires an infinitely small focal point and an infinitely large, multi-layered Cosmos (think about that one!).

6) The Cosmic Network is the *Framework* of the Cosmic Self; each point of consciousness within that Framework can attune itself to the Cosmic *Centre* (which is within everyone of us; and which is revealed once one has transcended Space and Time in one's consciousness).

7) Each one of us is a part of that Network; and collectively, on a Cosmic scale, we are the Network.

To take this in at its full face value is to open up the door within oneself which leads self to Self. Inasmuch as journeying facilitates this opening it can lead to transcendence.

(Further details regarding transcendence can be found in THE PSYCHIC EXPLORER and in STARCRAFT.)

What you have read so far and understood of your own accord is little more than an intellectual communication based on perspectives gleaned during moments of higher (-than-intellectual-) consciousness. The *Reality of the Cosmic Network* must be experienced directly, and it is essentially beyond intellectual consideration. Journeying is one of several methods which can place participants in contact with the Network, and with the Cosmic Self.

Taking up the 7th point above, that each one of us is part of the Network, whenever we act collectively — for instance, as a journeying group — we can access that Network as a group consciousness. The power of the encounter is spread, and it becomes easier to acknowledge and decipher the information along the chosen line of contact (i.e. a target, or what lies *behind* the target in terms of consciousness and intelligence). As the journeying group becomes more accustomed to dealing with that information it opens up new doors of realisation within the participants. The end result, if pursued at length, is transcendence.

If (and it is presently a big *if*) humanity participated in a collective journey the contacts which could be made would open up new doors for the whole of humanity, and our evolution as a humanity would be accelerated immeasurably. Since humanity has not yet achieved a more collective and holistic mode of consciousness it is forerunners, using methods such as journeying, who are in the position of opening up that contact; their efforts are automatically communicated, even if only subconsciously received, to everyone else, and bring about change, especially in consciousness.

All these considerations transcend the frameworks which we are normally accustomed to dealing with. They transcend politics, religions, philosophies, arts and sciences as we know them. They herald the true nature of what we call the *New Age*.

Also, the channel who guides a journey is channelling not only external flows of information, but an internal non-spacial gestalt. To the extent that the participants of a journey tune in to that level of reality there is no longer an external and an internal world — the two become coincident and reveal what lies beyond the apparent paradox involved: a metaphysical world where there is no separation in consciousness.

Whenever that state of consciousness is accessed the Reality of the *One Self* becomes absolutely clear and is acknowledged as intrinsic to the very nature of our Spiritual expression.

The roots of Life are seen and experienced as coincident with the evolutionary branching out and flowering achieved so far. By communicating/sharing with other subscribers to the Network we are can put ourselves in contact with other evolutionary branches and flowerings; collectively these branches and flowerings constitute the richness of Cosmic Evolution, affording new perspectives and new departures on an even greater Journey — the Journey of the Transcendent Spirit.

Once these points are assessed fully one realises that the Network is not only one of communication, but a System of Initiatic unfoldment — one initially set in motion by beings far more evolved than our human selves; beings of a Cosmic Order, to which we are in some way affiliated.

All Life is interdependent; each participant has hir potential role within the Network which favours the greater evolution of the whole. To the extent that we are in tune with Life's Evolution we are welcome subscribers to the Network and to all its benefits.

APPENDIX I

THE SEVEN PLANES & THE SEVEN COSMIC PLANES

Each of the Seven Planes is composed of seven sub-planes; and the Seven Planes collectively form the lowest of the Seven Cosmic Planes. Therefore one can say that there are 49 sub-planes within the Seven Planes, and 49 Planes within the Seven Cosmic Planes (or 343 sub-planes).

This system of Cosmic Planes is therefore absolutely vast, in fact well beyond our present comprehension: however the actual principle involved is relatively simple.

These are some of the names which are given to these levels (which names have been used in this book):

7th Plane: Adi (Systemic)
6th Plane: Monad (Seed-Self/One-Self)
5th Plane: Atma (Spiritual Will)
4th Plane: Buddhi (Harmonic; Spiritual Love)
3rd Plane: Higher Spiritual Mind, & Lower Mind: (Manas)
2nd Plane: Astral (The Dream Plane/emotional energy/sentiency)
1st. Plane: Etheric-physical Plane (the incarnational plane).

On the etheric-physical plane, dense solids, liquids and gases represent the three lowest sub-planes of matter.

The ancient Tibetans counted these Planes from the top.: ie the 1st Plane was the Adi; likewise with regard to the Cosmic Planes:

7th (1st) Cosmic Plane Of Adi
6th (2nd) Cosmic Plane Of Monad
5th (3rd) Cosmic Plane Of Atma
4th (4th) Cosmic Plane Of Buddhi
3rd (5th) Cosmic Mental Plane
2nd (6th) Cosmic Astral Plane
1st (7th) Cosmic etheric-physical Plane: i.e. the Seven Planes.

From one point of view all these Planes are in fact a spectrum: an infinite Spectrum! There are Meta-Cosmic Planes beyond the Cosmic Plane of Adi.

APPENDIX II

A — STARS AS SPIRITUAL BEINGS

The stars we see around us at night are the incarnations of Stellar Beings (and to them the Etheric-physical plane, as we know it, represents the equivalent of their densest sub-plane) — who have attained the evolutionary level which permits them to express themselves as stars. In this light a star represents an embodiment; by extension the whole of a solar system, including physical and non-physical planets, represents the greater embodiment of one such Stellar Being.

A physical star, such as the Sun, represents its densest embodiment; its *aura* extends well beyond the orbit of the furthest planet in its system. From another point of view a star is the *key* chakra within a given system, and each planet represents a secondary chakra and planetary Spiritual Being. The system works as a whole with a common purpose, and is affiliated with a group of stars — each with its own individual purpose within a greater group purpose.

This group or family of stars is affiliated in turn with other stellar groups, which together encompass an even greater purpose. Collectively all the stellar groups within a galaxy act out a galactic purpose; a galaxy is a Spiritual Being of a Higher Order.

There are also groups or families of galaxies, or Galactic Beings — these follow an even greater Purpose yet... and so on.

The interdependence of all these systems, from star systems to galaxies, to meta-galaxies (a huge grouping of galaxies, representing a Meta-Galactic Spiritual Being), stems from a common Purpose which is beyond our ken as human beings to understand fully, if much at all.

B — THE LOCAL FAMILY OF SUN-STARS

The Sun or Solar System is part of a specific family of stars, and fulfils a particular purpose within that group. Some of the other stars and systems belonging to this family are:

SIRIUS *A* — is 9 light years distant from the Sun, and is to be found in the constellation of Canis Major (The Greater Dog). Its physical light magnitude is 1.37 and its diameter is twice that of the Sun. It is prominent in the night sky, and can be seen clearly with or without the assistance of a telescope (if a telescope is tracked on Sirius *A* one can see flashing prismatic coloured lights; adjusting the lenses out of focus produces a ring of pulsing rainbow-coloured lights).

SIRIUS *B* — physically is a white dwarf star with a density 90,000 times greater than that of the Sun. It revolves once around Sirius *A* every 50 years, and it is a so-called *black hole*. Together Sirius *A* and *B* represent the *chief* system within the family to which the Sun belongs. It is referred to in esoteric traditions around the world; it is also referred to as the Dog Star, and as the "Great Instructor of mankind".

THE PLEIADES — physically, a group of seven newly-incarnated stars, all lying fairly close together in space in relative to apparent terms. Often referred to as the *Seven Sisters*, these can be found in the *neck* of the constellation of Taurus. Prominent stars: Alcyone, a white sub-giant. Merope is also of special visual interest, since the cloud of dust and gases around Merope reflect its light, forming a sort of blue halo — this also applies, if in slightly less spectacular way, to all the others. Estimated distance: 500 light years (although this figure does vary depending on which book you refer to!). In esoteric terms the Pleiades are referred to as the "Seven supposed wives of the seven Rishis of the Great Bear" (Ursa Major); also referred to as the Atlantides, and as the "feminine opposite of Brahma". (There are in fact 9 stars in that immediate vicinity: Alcyone, Merope, Electra, Maia, Taygeta, Atlas, Pleione, Celaeno and Asterope).

THE GREAT BEAR/URSA MAJOR/THE PLOUGH — familiar to all of us, its brightest star is Dubhe — a giant of spectral class K0, at a distance of 142 light years and with a magnitude of 1.95; a double star (or binary) system, of which the two components revolve around a common centre every 44 years. The other stars of this constellation are: Merak, 76 light years distant, with a magnitude of 2.44; Phekda, 80 light years distant; Megrez, 76 light years; Alioth, 78 light years; Benetnash, 163 light years; Mizar, 78 to 80 light years; and Alcor, 80 light years distant (the latter two appear in the sky as a single star — good eyesight can just about tell them apart — although Alcor is itself a binary system, so there are in fact three stars; there are a number of other stars in the overall constellation, however, and of note is Talitha). Referred to esoterically as the "Seven Rishis"; in Egypt it was referred to as the "Mother of Revolutions"; also referred to as Leviathan.

There are many other stars which are in direct to indirect interplay with our Solar System, on various levels, and more information on the esoteric aspects can be found in ESOTERIC ASTROLOGY by Alice A. Bailey (Lucis Press).

C — THE UNSEEN STARS

There are many stars around us which cannot be seen visually at the physical level; they are not in dense(st) physical incarnation, although some of them can be seen clairvoyantly on the etheric sub-levels of the etheric-physical plane. Their importance to us is masked to us, yet it is not by any means always inconsiderable. Other stars can be found in astral density, and some in mental density.

Stars, as Spiritual Beings, come and go from dense incarnation as we do. In a future time some of us may aspire to and become stars or planets in turn, while those Spiritual Beings who are stars now will embody the activity of much greater systems. In this manner the evolution of all Spiritual Beings ever grows towards the embodiment and expression of a higher system, and then the emancipation from that system.

D — HUMAN BEINGS AS STARS

Each one of us has a miniature replica of a solar system — the chakras which activate our expression, evolution and embodiment. Where we differ immeasurably from a solar system is in our ability to channel vast amounts of energy. A star, such as the Sun, *feeds* the whole Solar System, and if one considers the amount of energy which the physical Sun puts out to the system, compared with what we put out by way of energy as human beings, this indicates the measure of difference in our respective evolutions and states of consciousness as Spiritual beings — i.e. there is a considerable difference!

The principles involved are much the same, however. Each one of us is a *diminutive star* (and our *auras* form a sphere around us, which may extend from a few feet to several miles; the *aura* of Gautama Buddha, for instance, is said to have extended for three miles in radius).

There is a direct correspondence between the Seven Planes, in which we move, and the Seven Cosmic Planes, in which stars as Spiritual Beings move.

E — THE EVOLUTION OF SPIRITUAL BEINGS

A star, while embodying a particular Spiritual Being, is also composed and assisted by a vast amount of Spiritual beings, each one of which is part of a group with a specific purpose and activity within the system. All these beings evolve together, yet in some cases move from system to system as may be appropriate for their evolutions.

Not all beings become stars in their own right in the due course of their evolutions; nevertheless they may assist different groupings of stars in different ways.

Planets are *lesser stars* — i.e. not yet great or evolved enough to become outright stars. There has been speculation as to whether Jupiter might become a second star within the Solar System, nevertheless at the present time it has not yet got the necessary mass to draw enough material (systemic/cosmic dust and gases) to itself in order to ignite itself to the status of a fully fledged physical star. From an esoteric point of view it has not expanded its consciousness sufficiently to become an outright star. Should it do so in the future the Solar System would become a binary system.

While stars are *positively* or *negatively* polarised to each other (i.e. *male* or *female*, in relative terms), they are all androgynous, and partake of both main streams of evolution — *human* (type, which does not mean human as we know it, yet includes it) and devic. It is the fusion between the *human* and devic life-streams which permits stellar ignition. A star can be considered as a massive nuclear fusion reactor.

Stars evolve from proto-stars, and physically range from high temperature stars of type W, with a surface temperature of about 50,000 degrees Kelvin (blue-white stars), to relatively cool stars of type M, RN and S, with surface temperature of less than 3,500 degrees (red stars). Red stars are *dying stars*, yet some of these are enormous in size (and called red giants), such as Antares (Scorpius), Arcturus (Bootes), and Mirach (Andromeda). The diameter of Antares is 300 times greater than that of the Sun; Arcturus is 23 times larger.

Red giants eventually collapse and go nova, and the physical remnants become dwarf stars, with very low surface temperatures, or they become neutron stars, or so-called *black hole*, or they go supernova, in which case there is usually nothing left to be seen after they have exploded (or dematerialised, or disincarnated at the densest level).

Certain stars become *black holes* — i.e. highly dense stars, whose light cannot even escape into the surrounding space. Sirius *B*, which is a black hole, was only found astronomically because certain variations were detected in the *flight path* of Sirius *A*, which suggested that there must be a massive heavenly body nearby which nevertheless could not be seen optically. Subsequently Sirius *B* was identified as it occulted Sirius *A*, and the Sirius system was acknowledged as a binary system. Many esoteric traditions have always acknowledged the presence of Sirius *B*, despite the lack of telescopes in ancient times. While Sirius *B* is not a big star from the point of view of size, it is crushingly massive from the point of view of its density: 90,000 times that of the Sun.

The inner temperature of stars is far greater than that to be found on their surfaces; fusion temperatures are reached in the tens of millions of degrees Kelvin, and temperatures of 500 million degrees K are known to be possible.

There are other puzzling heavenly phenomena which we do not yet understand very well, such as quasi-stellar masses, or quasars. It is not yet clear what these are, and at one time they posed an enigma: their rate of rhythmic expansion and contraction appeared to take place at a speed greater than that of light (approx. 300,000kms), which is *impossible* in astrophysical terms.

There is an enormous amount that we do not yet know about stars, physically or Spiritually.

F — A COSMIC MASTER PLAN

There are many different points of view which can be held with regard to the nature of the Cosmos at a Spiritual to physical level, and these differentiations do not exclude an overall view.

1) Galaxies *emerge* into existence, first at a very high Spiritual Level, then progressively manifest themselves in ever-greater layers of density — this represents the involutionary stage of their manifestation (the descent of Spirit into *matter-state*); later the process is reversed, which heralds a gradual withdrawal from the dense layers — this is the evolutionary stage which eventually leads to their emancipation from the *matter-state;* from the point of view of a star, *matter-state* is represented by the seven Planes of the Cosmic Etheric-Physical Plane, i.e. that is its incarnational *zone* (see STARCRAFT for Devic information on all this).

2) All energy-matter *exploded* into existence at the moment of the *Big Bang*, and the galaxies formed themselves out of this material. This is currently the predominant astrophysical view. However, there may have been several *Big Bangs* in various locations of the Cosmos, and some of these may be taking place

at this very moment (from a physical stand-point we will not know anything about these until their particle emissions reach us in thousands to millions of years from now... if we are still around to witness them in any way); thirdly, *Big Bangs* may occur cyclically, and represent Cosmic Incarnations; fourthly, a *Big Bang* is the sudden emergence and manifestation of a Cosmic Entity on the lower Cosmic Levels, including the physical level; fifthly, the lower states of energy-matter are created progressively as manifestation takes place — i.e. they do not exist beforehand.

3) The *Steady State* theory posits that there is no *Big Bang* (or *Big Bangs*); from this position the Cosmos evolves out of itself, and galaxies form themselves and dissolve at intervals. (Are *Big Bangs* a Freudian slip, one wonders — a male perception? Versus the *Steady State* — a female perception?!)

4) There is a Matter and Anti-Matter Universe, or a *positive* and *negative* Universe, which are complementary. While it is now acknowledged that matter and anti-matter particles only *annihilate* each other whenever they encounter their exact *opposite partners*, as it were — e.g. an atom of matter-hydrogen and an atom of anti-matter-hydrogen will cancel each other out, while an atom of matter-hydrogen will not unduly affect an atom of anti-matter-carbon, etc — the *end* or physical death/disincarnation of the Universe would only take place when matter and anti-matter are drawn together in a precisely matching manner.

5) A *Master Plan* may exist, which regulates the emergence and withdrawal of Cosmic Consciousness from Cosmic Incarnation.

We could go on at some length with these and other considerations.

It remains that there is a Cosmic Network, and that all events within the Cosmos are part of a Greater Evolution and subject to a Greater Purpose than we can presently understand.

APPENDIX III

GLOSSARY OF TERMS

Some the terms mentioned below have not been used in the text of this book, nevertheless they are listed here for the sake of reference with regard to future and existing SPIRAL PUBLICATIONS (in this instance as published by Skoob Books Publishing Ltd).

ADI — the 7th Plane, also referred to as the Systemic Plane. At this level of reality and consciousness the whole Solar System is perceived as a single Being, of a certain Cosmic Order, with affiliations with certain other star systems of which it is a family member. (From a Spiritual point of view this is the 1st Plane.)

ASTRAL PLANE — the 2nd Plane (or 6th if viewed from a Spiritual angle); embodies the principles of sentiency and emotional response. The Astral Plane can be visited and experienced in consciousness by projecting astrally. It is also called the *Dream Plane* (see THE PSYCHIC EXPLORER).

ATMA/ATMIC PLANE — the Spiritual *Power Self*, or 1st Aspect of the Higher Self; the 5th Plane (or 3rd when viewed from a Spiritual angle), embodying the Principle of Power (1st Ray; from another angle, the 3rd Ray, but we won't go into that here).

BUDDHI/BUDDHIC PLANE — the Spiritual *Unitive Self*, or 2nd Aspect of the Higher Self; the 4th Plane, embodying the Principle of Union, Intuition, Love-Wisdom (2nd Ray), and also that of Harmony (4th Ray).

CONSCIOUSNESS — the faculty of evolving a greater contact with Life and a state of realisation which involves ever-increasing union with Spiritual Life. Consciousness is not a mental principle, however it uses the mind to assess the contents of encoded energy-information. Related to Spiritual Intuition. Seen from a certain viewpoint it evolves from the interaction of the Principles of Power (1st Ray, *Nagual*) and Mind (3rd Ray, *Tonal*), and is derived from the Principle of Union (2nd Ray, which is often referred to as the Ray of Love-Wisdom). It also called the *silent observer*; in the Castaneda books, particularly in THE POWER OF SILENCE, it is referred to as the point of *silent knowledge*.

COSMIC BEING — any Being of a Cosmic Order (see also COSMIC SELF and EVERNESS).

COSMIC PLANE — one of seven Cosmic Planes; the Cosmic Etheric-Physical Plane, or the Seven Planes as we know them, is the lowest, i.e. the densest in energy-matter terms.

COSMIC SELF — the Essential Being of which we and all other beings and things are a part.

DEVA — a term which refers to the various angelic races, some of which are directly complementary to the human and human-equivalent races (see SOLAR DEVA). Devas are the builders of Supernature and Nature, of the Planes, and of all the energies and structures/embodiments found thereupon, which they also maintain and nurture. From a certain point of view devas represent the *female* aspect of Life, and humans/human-equivalents represent the *male*.

DOOR/GATE — any access point or *switchboard* which permits the passage of consciousness from one level to another.

ELEMENTALS — diminutive devas, associated with atoms, which are always a part of an *elemental group*, including *fire, air, water, and earth* — on different levels.

EVERNESS — the highest known focus of the Cosmic Self (not directly accessible by human beings — by a long way — yet eventually accessed as a Cosmic Entity); a term used as a substitute for the Highest (known) Cosmic Being on the 7th Cosmic Plane (or 1st Cosmic Plane when viewed from the High-Spirit).

EXISTENCE — the transcendent and manifested nature of Life/Cosmic Self.

GESTALT — a state of mental and intuitive union.

HIGHER SELF — the Spiritual Self, embodied by the Spiritual Triad of Power, Love-Wisdom, & Mind — these being the three differentiated Aspects of the Monad (see MONAD).

LOWER SELF — the personality self, which is the *imperfected shadow* of the Higher Self, operating on the lower Mental, Astral and etheric-physical Planes (the latter is generally not looked upon as a principle, but only as a concretised effect). When the *shadow* becomes perfected it becomes fused with the Higher Self — this process adds the faculty of individuality to the Higher Self, which in itself is a representative of the Cosmic Self and therefore not otherwise individualised.

MANAS/MIND/MENTAL PLANE — the 3rd Plane, which is divided into two main areas: the lower personality/concrete mind, and the higher intellectual/abstract Mind, or 3rd Aspect of the Higher Self.

MONAD/MONADIC PLANE — the representative of the Cosmic Self within the seven Planes which we can access as human beings. Also referred to esoterically as the *Seed Self*. The Monad is first consciously accessed and acknowledged at the peak of the 1st Life-Initiation — which is a devastating, yet beautiful and highly revealing experience. The Monadic Plane is the 6th Level (2nd Spiritually), and after the individual self has finally gone through the process of transmutation and transcendence this Plane eventually becomes the *home* of the conscious Self — at the 5th Life-Initiation (from another point of view the lower self is a small fragment of the Monad which the latter projects down into density and cycles of incarnation in order to acquire certain abilities, including individuality — which latter is sometimes referred to as the *gift of the lower self to the Higher Self* to become a *gift* the individual must fuse hirself in consciousness with the Spirit).

ONENESS — a state of Spiritual Union; there are various levels of Oneness, each succeeding (or higher) one encompassing more of the Cosmic Reality and Cosmic Consciousness.

RAYS — there are 3 primary Rays, Power, Love/Wisdom and Creative Mind, and 4 secondary Rays (sub-aspects of the 3rd Ray): Harmony-through-conflict, Discriminating Mind, Ideas/Ideals, and Rhythmic Magick.

SOLAR DEVA — the part of Self which is complementary to the Spiritual human state, or Soul. A Solar Deva, while part of the overall Self, is a relatively independent being with which its human complement can fuse in consciousness, and thus regain a state of conscious androgyny.

SOLAR PITRI — a specific kind of Stellar Deva who is receptive to the energies and encoded energy-information emanating from other star systems, which it then modifies appropriately for use within its own star system. Lives and works with others within the Sun (or any other star).

SOUL — the part of Self (or Monad) which incarnates fractions of itself in order to harvest certain abilities under duress (a duress afforded by the lower or denser Planes, particularly during incarnation on the physical plane).

SPIRIT — a term which is used in a variety of ways, however in the context of this book it is used to refer to higher evolved Beings, higher consciousness, the Higher Planes, particularly the Atmic, Monadic, Adi or Adic/Adaic Planes. It is also called *Power*, or *Nagual*. The High-Spirit is the Cosmic Spirit — as related to the Higher Cosmic Planes.

SPIRIT TRIBE — a group or Race of Spiritual beings acting collectively; some Spirit Tribes are made up of several Spiritual groups.

TRANSCENDENCE — the act or process of evolving consciously out of the lower planes and permanently accessing ever-higher Levels of existence.

TRANSMUTATION — the change-over period and process which leads to transcendence, and away from the normal human state.

A COMMUNICATION

(A channelling to end this book. Source quoted as "Alpha-Zero".)

We note with interest the end of the writing of this book. It is up to those who will read it to make good sense of it, for while what you have to say opens up the door, there is much more to the art of channelling and journeying than is conveyed here.

Nevertheless, this is entirely as it should be. What we have to say here is simple, and yet to you — those who will read it — it may seem unbelievably complex.

The Network, as hinted at in this book, is vaster than you can possibly comprehend at this stage in your evolution; even an Adept has much difficulty in understanding it, and even then only partially. It would be simple enough if all you had to do was to consider the vast amount of stars that exist even in your own sector of your own small galaxy — but when you take into account that there are countless numbers of galaxies, and countless Planes of Existence (even the 49 Planes and 7 Cosmic Planes as outlined in the tabulation to be found in this book do not account for all that there IS), then you may yet wonder at the fullness of the Para-Cosmic Spectrum, and what may lie even Beyond That.

There is no end to Life. Those who have evolved to very high estates of thought-energy-intuition-and-Will in other kalpas and mahakalpas (cosmic periods of time) have done little more than open up certain doors for themselves, and thereby have also opened up doors for others — those who follow them, including eventually yourselves. You must understand that from a high position of view you yourselves are only just beginning to embark on the Cosmic Voyage or Journey — there is so much ahead of you that you can be forgiven for not understanding much of what we could put forward to you by way of impressions and knowledge. In fact, if we are to point out the obvious, what you use by way of exchange-information as language is so limiting to us whenever we might want to convey a truth to you that what we have to say is masked by the obtrusiveness of the words you use. Even in a state of *open telepathy* you would still not be able to understand much of what lies ahead of you.

When it comes to touching upon the Network, of which a small amount is conveyed through the medium of this book, you would need to stretch your perceptions almost immeasurably in order to take in what there is by way of planets and stars, and galaxies, and metagalaxies, and greater systems as yet unrecognised by you, and this on several Levels. Each planet/star/galaxy/metagalaxy, is a powerful being, and you yourselves, while powerful in a very small way, you cannot entirely comprehend just how powerful a sunstar truly is; the power of a galaxy is billions of times greater; the power of a meta-galaxy is not even approachable using the terms of reference you might care to invoke or invent. You cannot yet see how many different zones of beingness that a star *occupies* there are; and that its magnitude in Cosmic evolutionary terms is very small, regardless of how great its output may be in terms of life-expression.

What we want to put to you here is something which has not been mentioned in this book, and this is the factor of *hidden geometry*. The Network is not an amorphous connection-system between different stars and galaxies, not to mention all the other types of powerful beings which live and express themselves in the celestial spheres — there is a subtle, esoteric geometry which permits all these cosmic beings to intercommunicate and exchange energies and impressions along the strands of the Network; this geometry is not a physical one, therefore there is no point trying to work out how far this or that star might be from you, and from other stars — it is a *hidden geometry*, because it is not a spacial geometry.

Something for you to ponder upon.

The Network itself is multi-levelled, so much so that you would have to *see* it from a multiplicity of view-points and Plane-Levels in order to even vaguely perceive just how it is *built* and how it functions. Only an Initiate of a High Degree (such as a star) can even begin to understand and appreciate how it works and how it has been put together — out of the extensions of consciousness that stars — as beings — have put out into Meta-Space and Meta-Time, linking them together sometimes for the first time at a conscious level.

When you consider that what you consider to be space is but a small subset of Meta-Space, and that time as you know it is but an even smaller subset of Meta-Time, making both time and space as you know them seem entirely insignificant, even illusionary to us, then you may just start to intuit as to what is really *out there* — in the infinitely big expanse which we refer to as Meta-Time and Meta-Space; and there are magnitudes of Time and Space Beyond even these.

When you further consider that each planet and star, and each galaxy and metagalaxy, has its own *reach* — its own growth status or pattern and that each heavenly being has hir own particular *signature* in terms of evolutionary growth; and that the parts of each of those beings' evolution do not evolve in precisely the same way; and that some of these beings evolve faster than others; and that some develop their expression on one or several Levels in preference to others first, then tackle the rest later as may be convenient to them or necessary — then perhaps you may just begin to understand that the Network itself is full of complex ramifications — some Levels may be connected; others may not be, etc.

If you further think of this Network as something of a *nervous system*, and that during periods of (star) wakefulness this Network is buzzing with information and power-energies; and that during moments of (star) sleep these beings actually, in their own way, dream, and that their dreams are vastly different from your own, revealing to them as they do something of the contents and workings of their own Meta-Psyches; and that stars also Meditate, Journey and work Magick, and access what to them are States of Super-Conscious Reality — then, maybe, you will *see* something of the Relationship of Power which they share.

Further consider that there is no time — all things are happening simultaneously in a *Momentless Moment*. Thus, when Life is seen from this angle all beings are effectively *equal;* and yet those beings that we are referring to are greatly in advance of you on the Cosmic Scale of Consciousness-Evolution.

That is all that we wish to point out at this time.

ESSENTIAL BIBLIOGRAPHY

Carlos Castaneda:
THE TEACHINGS OF DON JUAN (Penguin)
A SEPARATE REALITY (Penguin)
JOURNEY TO IXTLAN (Penguin)
TALES OF POWER (Penguin)
THE SECOND RING OF POWER (Penguin)
THE EAGLE'S GIFT (Penguin)
THE FIRE FROM WITHIN (Century Publishing)
THE POWER OF SILENCE (Simon and Schuster)

Alice A. Bailey:
ESOTERIC ASTROLOGY (Lucis Press)
A TREATISE ON COSMIC FIRE (Lucis Press)
ESOTERIC PSYCHOLOGY — I (Lucis Press)
ESOTERIC PSYCHOLOGY — II (Lucis Press)
A TREATISE ON WHITE MAGIC (Lucis Press)
THE RAYS AND THE INITIATIONS (Lucis Press)
LETTERS ON OCCULT MEDITATION (Lucis Press)
ESOTERIC HEALING (Lucis Press)

Vee Van Dam:
THE PSYCHIC EXPLORER (Skoob Books Ltd., Spiral Publications)
THE POWER OF MIND & CONSCIOUSNESS (Skoob Books Ltd., Spiral Publications)
STARCRAFT (Skoob Books Ltd., Spiral Publications)

Richard Bach:
A BRIDGE ACROSS FOREVER (Pan)

Barbara Hand Clow:
EYE OF THE CENTAUR (Llewellyn Publications)

Steve Richards:
INVISIBILITY; MASTERING THE ART OF VANISHING (The Aquarian Press)

Robert A. Monroe:
JOURNEYS OUT OF THE BODY (Corgi)

G.M. Glaskin:
WORLDS WITHIN (Arrow)

Fritjof Capra:
THE TAO OF PHYSICS (Fontana)

Lyall Watson:
SUPERNATURE (Coronet)

Neil F. Michelsen:
THE AMERICAN EPHEMERIS FOR THE 20TH CENTURY (ACS Publications)

G.A. Briggs and F.W. Taylor:
THE CAMBRIDGE PHOTOGRAPHIC ATLAS OF THE PLANETS (Cambridge U. Press)

Josef Klepesta and Antonin Rukl:
CONSTELLATIONS (Hamlyn)

Timothy Ferris:
GALAXIES (Sierra Club; Stewart, Tabori & Chang)

Michael Tobias:
DEVA (Avant Books; Fiction)

Ingo Swann:
STAR FIRE (Sphere; Fiction)

Jane Roberts:
THE EDUCATION OF OVERSOUL SEVEN (Prentice-Hall Inc.; Fiction)

Forthcoming titles in the SKOOB ESOTERICA series

Kenneth Grant: The Carfax Monographs
Explorations of the origins and potential of myth and magick, illustrated by Steffi Grant.

Victor B. Neuburg: The Triumph of Pan
Originally published by Aleister Crowley's Equinox Press in 1910.
(facsimile limited edition)

Michael Harrison: The Fire from Heaven
Explores the evidence for spontaneous human combustion and summarises the evidence.

Three books by **Vee Van Dam**:

The Psychic Explorer
Concerned with astral projection and out of body experience

Starcraft
Discovering auric energies and working with devas.

Vivienne Browning: The Uncommon Medium
The story of the Paracelsian Vyvyan Deacon told by his daughter.

E. Graham Howe: The Mind of the Druid
Meditations on the elemental origns of human psychology and faith.